FOREWORD BY **RYAN STEWMAN**

MILLION DOLLAR IDENTITY

**Experts, CEOs, and Entrepreneurs
Share How to Build, Monetize, and
Scale Your Market Authority, Profit,
and Influence for 7+ Figure Success**

**MYRON GOLDEN, Ph.D.
VICTORIA KENNEDY
DAN ASHBURN
KIANA DANIAL
ERIC BEER**

Million Dollar Identity

Experts, CEOs, and Entrepreneurs Share How to Build, Monetize, and Scale Your Market Authority, Profit, and Influence for 7+ Figure Success

Written by Myron Golden, Ph.D. © 2022, Victoria Kennedy © 2022, Dan Ashburn © 2022, Kiana Danial © 2022, Eric Beer © 2022, Jamie Wolf © 2022, Keenan Williams © 2022, Dr. Hermanie Pierre © 2022, Kelly Jefferson © 2022, Teresa Harding © 2022, The Kitti Sisters © 2022, Galen M. Hair © 2022, Jay Altman © 2022, Chris Clear © 2022, Barry Gabster © 2022, Robert Nickell © 2022, Lori Lynn © 2022, Angela Little © 2022, James Golden © 2022, Ariel Amavi © 2022

Copyright of the Collective Work, Jamie Wolf LLC © 2022

Wolf Tide Publishing, Beaufort, SC © 2022

Print ISBN: 978-1-938953-34-7

Disclaimer: This book is for educational purposes only. All views, thoughts, and opinions expressed by any author belong solely to that author. They do not reflect or represent those of Million Dollar Story Agency, its parent company, Jamie Wolf LLC, Jamie Wolf, or any of the other individual authors, their companies, affiliates, or organizations represented in any volume of *Million Dollar Story.*

Any content provided by a *Million Dollar Story* author is of their opinion and is not intended to malign any religion, ethnic group, race, gender, club, organization, company, individual, or anyone or anything. Additionally, all writers' opinions are their own and do not constitute financial, business, or health advice in any way whatsoever, nor should any content be relied upon for investment or medical decisions.

The authors' opinions, material, training, and offers are based upon information they consider reliable but neither Million Dollar Story Agency, nor its parent company or affiliates, with which such authors are affiliated, warrant its completeness or accuracy, and it should not be relied upon as such.

Million Dollar Story Agency strongly recommends that you do your own due diligence, perform your own independent research, and/or speak with a qualified professional before making any investment, business, medical, financial, or health decisions.

The reader is responsible for his or her own actions. Adherence to all applicable laws and regulations, including international, federal, state, and local governing professional licensing, business practices, advertising, and all other aspects of doing business in the United States, Canada, or any other jurisdiction is the sole responsibility of the purchaser or reader. Neither the author nor the publisher assumes any responsibility or liability whatsoever on the behalf of the purchaser or reader of these materials.

DEDICATION

To all of you who choose faith, resilience, courage, perseverance, and
curiosity to see who you might *become* when you
embrace growth and joy.

Day by day,

what you choose,

what you think,

and what you do

is who you become.

Heraclitus c.540–c.480 BC

OTHER BOOKS AVAILABLE FROM WOLF TIDE PUBLISHING

Million Dollar Story Volume 1

Million Dollar Story Volume 2

Million Dollar Moms

Million Dollar Dads

Million Dollar Method

Start Over Start Now, Ten Keys to Success in Business and Life

Start Over Start Now Guidebooks 1-10: Make Decisions, Take Action, Fail Frequently, Listen Intently, Develop Yourself, Practice Balance, Get Healthy, Network Authentically, Attract Money, Give Back

How to Be a Successful Entrepreneur Volume 1

How to Be a Successful Entrepreneur Volume 2

Learn more here:
milliondollarstory.co

CONTENTS

FOREWORD

RYAN STEWMAN

Identity is a shapeshifter.

You start out as someone else's son or daughter.

Then, later, you identify yourself as a class clown or a star student or a jock or a geek.

But what if your identity takes a sudden shift? What if you find yourself being identified as a trouble maker … a rule-breaker … a criminal … a reject … a felon.

Then what?

Adopted at 7, a high school dropout at 15, and a felon at 20, I wasn't born with a Million Dollar Identity. I created it. By the time I turned 25, I had become a millionaire.

But I didn't stay there.

I ended up serving more time (this time wrongfully) and losing everything—my livelihood, my wife, my house, my freedom. I started over again on July 8, 2008, believing I had it in me to gain it all back and then some.

You need to understand something. You—and you alone—have the power to change your stars. To forge a new identity. To dare to believe that anything is possible. To make the impossible possible.

You don't have to accept what other people tell you that you are. YOU decide who you are and then you go figure out how to become that person.

Every day, I strive to become the best version of myself I can be. Every day, I follow the <G>CODE. Because of that, today, I'm married to the most amazing woman on the planet. Together, we have four magnificent children. We've coached more than 17,000 students in our coaching program, and we have over two million followers. Every day, without fail, I show up.

Every day, I fight the Force of Average.

To attain a Million Dollar Identity, you have to understand your enemy. It's not your parents. It's not your teachers. It's not your boss. It's not your spouse. It's not even you. It's the Force of Average.

And you've got to prepare for battle every single day of your life, armed to the hilt, giving your excuses the finger, and showing up consistently and persistently in four key areas of your life. (If you want to know each of those areas and what I do to continually press toward becoming the most elite version of myself that I can be, then pick up the book <G>CODE after you read this book.)

Every single person in this book has a Million Dollar Identity. They've found the one thing that has catapulted their success. Some of them are my friends. Some have gone through my coaching programs and are forcing me to run harder just to keep up.

They're all A-players. High achievers. Peak performers. But they all started out as infants who went on to become teenagers who messed up enough as adults to finally make their way from trouble maker to world changer.

Whatever your identity is right now doesn't matter. Take it from an ex-felon turned four-time bestselling published author. You get to choose your own identity.

Each story in this book is probably similar to your own story in some way. Find the key that puts you on a winning trajectory.

It's time to unlock the code to your Million Dollar Identity.

—**Ryan Stewman**, Owner/Founder of nine multi-million-dollar companies, four-time best-selling author, creator of DailyGCode app, host of the *ReWire Podcast*

ADVANCE PRAISE

Step outside your comfort zone, find a mentor, work like hell, accept that you'll make dumb mistakes, and you will find yourself wearing and owning a Million Dollar Identity just like the highly sought-after entrepreneurs in these chapters.

Learn from them, make a plan, and do the work to deliver value and help people; you, too, will have all that comes with a Million Dollar Identity.

—**Frank Kern**, FrankKern.com

Do you desire to improve your circumstances and change your life for the better? Have you tried so many approaches that your dream is starting to feel hopeless? Well, I have some good news for you. When you understand what it takes to develop a Million Dollar Identity then you're well on your way to the life you've always dreamed of. No matter where you are now, there is a path for you to achieve a Million Dollar Identity! I believe that this book could be a very big step in the direction you've been seeking to go.

—**Joel Bauer**, JoelBauer.com

Do you believe that if you've attended the School of Hard Knocks you can graduate with a Million Dollar Identity? I've spent a lifetime living on the edge of my comfort zone and loving every opportunity life has to offer. In the following pages you will read stories of successful, wealthy, accomplished entrepreneurs who began where you are today. Whether life was pretty normal until some catalyst changed things for them, or life was one challenge after another, each made a decision that is available to you now. They decided to BE somebody so they could have and do more, for themselves, their families, their communities, and those they serve and teach. Now it's your turn to read, be inspired, choose to be a trailblazer like me, and step into your Million Dollar Identity!

—TGo (Theresa Goss), Bestselling Author and National TV Talk Show Host, TGo.ExpertTalkWithTGO.com

Intelligence, talent, hard work, and resources alone cannot build a $100 million business or change the lives of millions. The key to achieving what many will say is impossible begins with mindset and adopting the right identity. Regardless of where you begin your journey—whether that's competing for a spot in the world's most elite special forces unit, flipping a business-ending disaster to a strategic advantage, or securing and generating the funds to launch and scale a billion-dollar brand—taking on a Million Dollar Identity determines your ultimate results and the pure enjoyment of the game. When you are willing to hold big visions for what can be accomplished and partner with the right mentors, as the entrepreneurs in these pages have done, you can achieve $1 billion in sales or redefine how great brands are built, as I have been able to do.

—Tom Shipley, TShipley.com

Having a Million Dollar Identity starts with your mind, belief, and commitment to achieving your goals. This book is the GPS to help you build a strategy for earning a 6- and 7- figure income and achieve your Million Dollar Identity.

—Nehemiah Davis, MastermindWithND.com

PREFACE

If you are an entrepreneur who has become a leader, then you know what it's like to leave safety and familiarity. You have cycled through succeeding, falling, and then rising again. You may have thought you were on a quest in one direction, only to grow and uncover a deeper purpose and a new identity. Today, you no longer identify with your old normal.

This book exists to explore and share stories of real entrepreneurs who have become more than the revenue they earn. They have become the inspirational leaders who mentor and guide the next generation of heroes, leading them to uncover their new identity—*your* new identity. Your Million Dollar Identity.

Regardless of your background and the events that have unfolded for you on your journey so far, how do you build a million-dollar business and beyond? Who do you become on your journey to reach the point where it's no longer about the money? Importantly, what does that mean for those in your circle—your family, your community, your clients, your customers—and what does it mean for your purpose and legacy when you acquire a Million Dollar Identity?

Read on!

INTRODUCTION

Myron Golden is fond of saying you can earn $1 million dollars if you get paid $25,000 annually—but it will take you forty years! Chances are, however, you won't feel like a millionaire at that point.

In the following pages, you will meet individuals who have chosen to forego a steady paycheck in the employment of others. Instead, they have accepted the challenge to be uncomfortable, to grow into a person who can generate $1 million in revenue in five years or five weeks—or even in one day.

They, like you, experienced pain or frustration. They were afraid and ran into barriers that held them back and prevented them from achieving big dreams. Then, something happened and they were faced with a choice that changed everything ... but perhaps not the way they anticipated.

Today they are successful in all the ways our society measures such things, but that was not always the case. I understand it's easy to feel that people who seem to have health, wealth, and love in their lives acquired those with ease and speed. I've felt that way, too, wondering how I might live such a life. What I've found, and what the entrepreneurs will share with you in the following pages, is that there are many ways to reach our desires, dreams, and goals—but one thing is certain: we don't get there alone. We rely on other people to be our guides and our mentors, so that their learned and earned experience becomes ours.

You may not be a millionaire today. Or maybe you have just broken through to seven figures and now want to crack the code to get to eight or nine figures to serve more people and use your affluence to influence positive change. Wherever you are today, I guarantee you will acquire a Million Dollar Identity when you surround yourself with people who have been where you are and can show you what's possible. Know without a doubt your dreams are possible. The life you desire is possible. We see you, and we collectively are here to cheer for you on your way to your Million Dollar Identity.

Find your guide and begin your journey now.

CHAPTER ONE

MYRON GOLDEN, Ph.D.

Myron Golden, Ph.D.

Myron Golden teaches everyday people to become wealthy. The author of several books on the subjects of business and finance, Myron has assisted his clients in building businesses that do as much as $10 million per year in revenue.

He contracted polio as an infant (the result of being born in a segregated hospital), walks with a limp, and wears a brace on his left leg. None of that stopped him from attaining a black belt in karate. Today he plays golf as often as possible and resides in Tampa, Florida, with his beautiful wife Tonie.

About 12 years ago, while teaching financial literacy and business success secrets from a biblical perspective, he says he made the greatest discovery he had ever made up to that point, which is the secret to attaining a Million Dollar Identity.

A coveted speaker in business and marketing circles, Myron travels and speaks internationally, sharing his timeless wisdom. One of his superpowers is being able to turn millionaires into multimillionaires.

FROM MILLION DOLLAR FANTASY TO MILLION DOLLAR REALITY

Millions of people have had the thought, "I would like to be a millionaire." Or they've thought, "I'd like to have a million dollars." But what does it *take* to "be a millionaire" or "have a million dollars"?

The answer to those questions is what this book is all about. And amazingly enough, it has nothing to do with winning the lottery or receiving an inheritance from a rich relative.

If you are serious—not just curious—about turning your million-dollar fantasy into a million-dollar reality, then you must first adopt the Million Dollar Identity.

Until you own the Million Dollar Identity, you will never be able to do the million-dollar activities. Until you're able to do the million-dollar activities, you will never be able to own the million dollars' worth of property, whether that property is real estate, intellectual property, or other valuable assets.

In other words, you can't have the result of a million-dollar reality until you do the activity that can earn a million dollars, and you won't be able to do the activity that can earn a million dollars until you own the identity.

Each author who has contributed a chapter to this book possesses a Million Dollar Identity. As each author pulls back the curtain on their own unique identities, they will show you what they have discovered, developed, and deployed to make their dreams a reality.

Let's start by laying a foundation. If you'll allow me, the first thing I'd like to bring to your attention is a concept that will bring clarity and connection to your mind.

You may have been taught (as I was) that if something isn't working, you need to just "try harder!" But "trying harder" isn't the key to successful outcomes. "Trying harder" is nothing more than putting more energy into an input that has no ability to create the output you desire.

The truth is, if you want to change the *output*, you must first change the *input*.

Inputs create outputs.

If you want to change the output for anything, you don't change the output by putting more energy into attempting to change the output. The only way to change the output is to change the input.

If you change the input, the output changes automatically.

For example, if you change the seed you plant in the ground, you get a different harvest. If you want a cup of coffee, you don't steep tea bags. If you want eggs for breakfast, you don't reach for oatmeal.

Now let's take a look at which inputs produce which outputs when it comes to turning those million-dollar fantasies into million-dollar realities.

If you desire to change what you have in your life—any output, result, outcome, or payoff—you have to change what you put in. But most people go about it the wrong way. And that's why becoming a millionaire never works for them.

For example, can you imagine if every time you went to put on your shoes, you attempted to put your left shoe on your right foot and your right shoe on your left foot? If you did that every time, then shoes would never work for you, right?

Can you imagine if every time you got in your car to drive it, you got in the back seat, reached over the front seat, and started the car? Driving a car would never work for you.

What has to happen is that you've got to wake up to the idea that for you to do what it takes to become a millionaire, you have to do the *right* things—and not only do the right things but also do them in the right order.

Since our attention is naturally drawn to what we would like to *have*, most people put all of their attention on *having*. But I am telling you that if you focus on having a better car, house, income, job, relationship, life ... if you focus on "the *having*," you're always going to find yourself frustrated and empty at the end of the adventure, whatever that adventure happens to be.

People desire to *have*, so they attempt to *do* X, Y, and Z, but they bump their heads on their inability to do it. Without the ability to do the thing, you cannot have the stuff.

So how do you get the ability to do the thing so you can have the stuff? You do it by first *becoming* the person who can do the thing who can then have the stuff. You see, "being" precedes "doing" and "doing" precedes "having." That's how God set it up from the beginning.

Let's go back to the laws of physics for a moment. God established a platform for us to operate on from the beginning of time, and that is how we experience life on planet earth. That platform is TIME | SPACE | MATTER.

If we are going to operate on this platform, anything that we do (that is going to work) is going to have to work within the boundaries of time, space, and matter. A lot of people don't like the words "boundaries," "rules," "laws," or "principles," but the reality is that freedom can only exist inside of boundaries.

If there are no boundaries, there can be no freedom. What does that mean? Well, can you imagine if you came home one day and your neighbor was sitting in your chair, eating your ice cream out of your freezer?

The conversation might go something like this:

"Whoa, wait, dude, what are you doing? This is my house."

"Eh, your house, my house, our house, his house, her house. Who cares? It's just a house, right?"

That's not acceptable.

The reason we have walls and doors on our houses is to establish boundaries. A boundary says that there are things I can do in here that I can't do out there. And certain people are allowed in here while other people have to stay out there.

Freedom exists inside of boundaries. I can go anywhere I want inside my own house. I can go upstairs or downstairs and sit in any chair I want, but I can't just go into my neighbor's house, walk in the front door, and sit in his chair—I might get shot!

It's important to understand that God set up some boundaries for how things work, so if you're going to do things and you desire for them to work for you, you have to operate within these three boundaries: TIME | SPACE | MATTER.

That is the platform. And it's the same for everyone. There are no exceptions.

On that platform, God set up some parameters. The parameters are: BE | DO | HAVE. Now that's a clue. Because those parameters teach us something else ...

Don't be? Can't do.

Can't do? Can't have!

Be a little ... Do a little ... Have a little.

Be a lot ... Do a lot ... Have a lot!

This formula is about to get really good and really clear ...

What's cool about BE | DO | HAVE is that "being" takes place on the platform of TIME. "Doing" takes place on the platform of SPACE. And "having" takes place on the platform of MATTER.

The reason time exists is so we can, over time, become the person who can *do the thing*. And the reason space exists is so that we have *room* to do the thing. The reason matter exists is so that we can have the reward for doing the thing. Matter is also the *reward* for *becoming the person* who can *do the thing*.

What's interesting is that our greatest desire is *to have*. But God's greatest desire is for us to *become*.

The bridge between *being* and *having* is *doing*.

Now let's talk about the inputs, outputs, and gaps within the parameters of BE | DO | HAVE.

BE is the input for DO, and DO is the output for BE, while DO is the input for HAVE, and HAVE is the output for DO.

$$BE \rightarrow DO \rightarrow HAVE$$

One of the most amazing discoveries I've ever made in my life is understanding that every human being is already doing 100% of everything they are capable of doing while they are walking and working in their current identity.

If we desire to do more than we are doing right now (and to do more than we were doing in the past), then we have to *become* more than we are *being* right now, and we have to *become* more than we've been *being* in the past. Then, and only then, will we ever *do* more than we've been *doing* and *have* more than we've ever had in the past.

Being is the arena of our *identity*, which operates on the platform of TIME.

Doing is the arena of our *activity*, which operates on the platform of SPACE.

Having is the arena of our *property*, which operates on the platform of MATTER.

Being is the identity piece. Your identity dictates your activity; this means activity pours out of identity. You will only do the things that are consistent with who you see yourself as being.

People want to have all of the stuff that goes with their million-dollar fantasy—the fancy cars or the mansion on the hill or the big bank account. But the million-dollar fantasy will remain a fantasy until you own the Million Dollar Identity. Then, and only then, will you be able to comprehend and carry out the million-dollar activities that will earn you the million-dollar reality.

If you try to *have* without *doing*, you're living in a fantasy. If you try to *do* without *being*, you are living in frustration. Only when you *become* the person who *can* do and who *does* do the thing will you live a life of fulfillment. That's why the concept of the Million Dollar Identity is so important.

Identity produces activity, and activity produces property. Got that?

Now, let's look at how this applies in physics because there are some universal laws of nature that govern everything.

There's the law of energy (everything is energy). Energy is neither created nor destroyed; it just changes form.

There's the law of entropy. Anything left to itself tends to move more and more toward disorder. That's why you have to read books and intentionally grow your mind.

If you only do the things that come naturally, you are, over time, going to become worse and worse. If you don't make your body move—if you don't exercise—then your body deteriorates.

You have to allow yourself to be acted upon by an outside force because anything left to itself tends to move more and more toward disorder. That's the second law of thermodynamics.

If you don't weed the garden, the weeds will take over. If you don't take a bath, you will soon smell very, very bad. If you don't brush your teeth, eventually your teeth will decay and fall out of your head.

Everything has to be maintained and improved because if you're not improving things, then they are naturally deteriorating. Because of entropy, going backward requires no intention. It simply requires a lack of intention to go forward. Withdrawing, becoming more disconnected, smaller, weaker, or poorer—these are the natural results of a lack of effort.

Let's not forget the next law: the law of polarity. For every action, there is an equal and opposite reaction. For every negative, there is a positive, and for every positive, there is a negative. It is impossible for something good to be in your life without the same amount of bad being in your life, which means it's also impossible for something bad to be in your life without the same amount of good.

Think about it … Have you ever seen a one-sided coin, a one-sided piece of paper, or a one-sided pancake? No, of course not! Why? Because it can't exist. It is impossible for anything to exist without two sides. That's where our choice comes into play. We get the side we focus on, but both sides are there all the time.

Are you with me?

If you've got a good thing in your life, that good thing in your life has a very bad side. But if you're focused on the good, then that's the part you're cultivating. You're becoming an outside force and acting upon the part of the thing that you desire to grow.

If you're focused on the positive, the positive cultivates, and the negative fades into the shadows. It's not that it no longer exists. It's just so out of focus that it doesn't distract or bother you anymore.

I'd be doing you a disservice if I didn't make you aware of the fact that your identity, your activity, and your property all have two sides as well. The negative of these three attributes is your current experience in reality. The positive of these three attributes is what you have the potential to BE, DO, and HAVE. In between the negative and the positive is a gap. That gap is your capacity.

Capacity is the difference between who you are now and who you could become. And capacity means that you can become more than you already are.

How do you fill the capacity gap?

You fill the capacity gap with *intentionality*.

For you to *become* more than you've been *being*, so that you can *do* more than you've been *doing*, so that you can *have* more than you've been *having*, you have to be *intentional*.

Intentionality requires discipline, focus, and resolve. The reason intentionality is so hard for most people is that the cultural-hypnotic-societal mechanism (what I call the media) programs us from the time we are small children to focus on distractions. By distractions, I mean anything that we give our attention to that doesn't make our lives, the lives of other people, or the world (in part or in whole) better.

We watch people on the electronic income reducer (what I call the TV) live their dreams while we are trapped in a nightmare. We wear jerseys with other people's names, teams, and numbers on our back, and we get excited when "our team" wins the game. But not a single person on "our team" even knows we exist.

We argue with people over things we saw or heard on the news even though the average so-called journalist doesn't spend any time at all checking facts. And most people never read a book or take a class to *intentionally* figure out how to make their lives better.

When you decide to focus on *intention* instead of *distractions*, you can discover your true identity. When that happens, look out world! Your impact is about to grow in a very real and dynamic way.

Right now, everything that you desire in your life that you don't currently have, you don't have because you don't know who you are. You've never discovered your true identity. If you don't know who you are, you can't know what you can do. If you don't know what you can do, you will never even attempt to do it. If you never do what you can do, you will never have what you *could* have.

You've not yet discovered who you really are.

You think you are who your parents, teachers, sibling, friends, or someone other than God told you that you are. And many times, they often told you who you're *not*. *You're not talented. You're not athletic. You're not attractive. You're not wanted. You're not capable. You're not smart. You're not … (fill in the blank).*

If somebody you looked up to told you who you are, with more emphasis on who you are not, and you bought into that identity, you will never maximize your true potential.

Today you may be operating based on that identity, but it's just something that somebody said to you when you were a child. You think you are who they said you are. You're buying into the identity lie, owning an identity that somebody gave you back in the third grade—someone who may not have had your best interest in mind.

Most of the frustration you have in your life is the result of not knowing who you truly are. Many people don't even realize that their sense of overwhelm comes from not developing themselves into their true identity. You have to be intentional about who you are being and who you are becoming.

Becoming the person who has a Million Dollar Identity means changing your identity from the person someone told you that you are (or are not) to the person you were created to be. Most people don't even realize how great they already are and the great things they would be able to do if they could only recognize who they truly are.

If you want more than you currently have, you need to change your activity. But you won't change your activity by doing something that goes against the person you believe yourself to be.

Identity is the input for activity.

Identity produces activity. Just like your identity has a gap, your activity also has a gap. That gap is the difference between what you are doing and what you could be doing.

In the same way that you use intentionality to fill the gap in your identity, you use ingenuity to fill the gap in your activity. Ingenuity is your willingness to keep creating new solutions until one of them works.

As Thomas Edison said, "I have not failed. I've just found 10,000 ways that won't work." Then he found a way that worked.

Sir Edmund Hillary famously said to the mountain after he first failed to successfully climb Mt. Everest, "You won't get any bigger, but we will, and we will keep coming until we are successful."

The gap in your activity is your ability. People often think that just because they don't currently know how to do something, that means they can't do it. But not knowing how to do something doesn't mean they can't do it—it just means they can't do it *yet*.

Why? Because they've not yet developed their identity into the person who can do that activity.

When you own an identity that practices intentionality, your activity will cause you to develop ingenuity that will help you find an answer or solution to any problem you will ever face.

I remember when I was a child in elementary school, working on an old raggedy car with my dad. We were attempting to remove a rusted bolt from the engine, and I said, "It's not coming out."

He said something to me that has stuck with me for my entire life. He said, "Oh, it's going to come out because we have a brain and it doesn't have a brain."

When you understand that you have an advantage over any problem you will ever face because you have a brain and it doesn't have a brain, it will change everything for you.

Do you know what else doesn't have a brain? Property. And your property is the direct result of your activity, which is the direct result of your identity. Property consists of the things you own: your net worth, your bank accounts, your art collections, your houses, your cars, your planes, your trains, your automobiles, your relationships, your health. All of these are things that you possess.

The gap between the property that you *could* have and the property you *do* have is called your opportunity. Opportunity is the difference between what you have and what you could have.

How do you fill that gap?

You fill the gap of opportunity with intensity. So you take your intentionality, you tie it to your ingenuity, and then you add your intensity, and now you've successfully started filling the gaps in your life.

Your intentionality causes you to focus on inputs and outcomes. Your ingenuity helps you find what works and how it works. And your intensity helps you focus only on desirable outcomes until you finish what you intended to do.

When you fill the gaps, it changes you. It changes your identity, which changes your activity, which changes your property. But it all starts with identity.

Now that you know *how* to fill the gaps, let's talk about *what you use* to fill them.

You fill the capacity gap in your identity by using your mindset. For example, intentionality is a mindset. Determination and gratitude are also mindsets.

You fill the potentiality gap in your activity by using your skillsets. Ingenuity is a skillset that gives you the ability to look at something, decipher what's wrong with it, and then fix it.

And you fill your property gap in your opportunity by using your toolsets. Intensity is a toolset that helps you capitalize on your opportunities.

If you take mindset, plus skillset, plus toolset, that equals assets. And income follows assets. The more assets you have, the more income you have.

Then, and only then, will you go from million-dollar fantasy to million-dollar reality.

Remember, though, it all starts with identity. If you get that input right, eventually you will develop the activity that causes you to deserve the property. That is why the Million Dollar Identity is the key that unlocks a cascade of growth and potential that seems miraculous from the outside looking in but seems effortless from the inside looking out.

Remember …

BE speaks to **Identity**. The Identity gap is called **Capacity**.

You fill the gap of Capacity with *Intentionality*.

That's your **MINDSET**.

DO speaks to **Activity**. The Activity gap is called **Potentiality**.

You fill the gap of Potentiality with *Ingenuity*.

That's your **SKILLSET**.

HAVE speaks to **Property**. The Property gap is called **Opportunity**.

You fill the gap of Opportunity with *Intensity*.

That's your **TOOLSET**.

Add your Mindset to your Skillset and your Skillset to your Toolset, and you can create **ASSETS**.

Mindset + Skillset + Toolset = ASSETS

The problem with most people is they think they want to become a millionaire, but what they really want is to have a million dollars. They're not the same thing. Having a million dollars is the result of becoming a millionaire, but becoming a millionaire is not the result of having a million dollars.

In this book, all of the authors (some of whom are my friends, and some of whom are my students) will be sharing their ideas and strategies on the Million Dollar Identity. We all took very different paths, but that is because we all come from very different starting points.

Give all of the authors in this book your attention and your *intention,* and allow yourself to be amazed as each one introduces you to a path that has the potential to lead you to your very own Million Dollar Identity.

If you want to learn more about what it means to have a Million Dollar Identity and scale your business exponentially, get my new book *B.O.S.S. Moves: Business Optimization Success Secrets from a Million Dollar Round Table* by going to:

BossMovesBook.com

CHAPTER TWO

VICTORIA KENNEDY

Victoria Kennedy

Victoria Kennedy is the CEO of Victorious PR, an award-winning, multi-million-dollar PR firm serving more than 100 clients around the world. A Two Comma Club award winner and TEDx speaker, she has also been voted CEO of the Year. She has been featured in over 200 publications, including *Forbes* and *Rolling Stone*. Victorious PR was voted Best PR firm in Las Vegas by Expertise.com, and they landed a spot on Clutch's list of top PR firms in Nevada. Named a "Cultural Leader" by *Rolling Stone* magazine, Victoria has also given talks, workshops, and has worked as a trusted consultant for entrepreneurs, C-level executives, and top Inc. 5,000 companies.

PENNILESS OPERA SINGER TO PR POWERHOUSE: REINVENT YOURSELF TO COMMAND ULTIMATE MARKET DOMINATION

Fear and anguish rush over me as I contemplate the meaning of what I had just read: *"Votre visa a été refusé."* I sit staring in disbelief at the letter in front of me:

"Your visa has been denied."

While on a routine trip to America to renew my visa, I received this earth-shaking letter from the French embassy with those words, now forever etched in my brain. My life as I knew it was now over. French officials refused to renew my visa, and there was no way to appeal their decision.

Without a chance to put my European affairs in order, all I had to my name was a small, carry-on suitcase of clothes I had brought with me to the U.S. How could I have known I would be stranded in a country that I hadn't called home in nearly three years? It was the most alone and invisible I have ever felt.

Fortunately, in my darkest hours, I wasn't totally alone. I had some generous friends living in the States who offered to take me in, and I quickly rented a small room in Las Vegas, which served as headquarters while I considered my next steps.

There was only one problem.

I had absolutely no idea what my next step would be.

From where I was sitting, I had only one real skill—singing opera. For two and a half years, I had been living a dream. As a professional opera singer, I bounced between Holland and France, singing in one beautiful castle or cathedral after another. I sang with opera greats like the renowned Italian tenor, Andrea Bocelli. And I even had a #1 hit single on the classical charts in Europe.

But now, a dark nightmare threatened to take it all away, shattering my dream career.

And it wasn't as if there were jobs for professional opera singers growing on trees, especially not in Sin City. Given the fact that I had just witnessed how precarious my position as an opera singer was, I wasn't exactly chomping at the bit to go back to that life.

No. I was ready to reinvent myself.

Still, reinvention seemed like a daunting task. If I knew then what I know now, which is that every millionaire, billionaire, and Fortune 500 CEO experiences a period (or many periods) of reinvention, I might have felt less hopeless in those early days. But I was far too deep into panic mode to think that clearly.

All I knew was that I needed to figure out my next move, and it had to be right now. So I started reading every book I could get my hands on about working for myself, learning digital skills, and marketing.

My first foray into starting my own business was real estate marketing. Why real estate? I don't have a profound answer to that question. I wasn't a huge HGTV fan. (I didn't even own a television.) I didn't have a deep-seated yearning to help "the real housewives" of Las Vegas market their homes to an audience I didn't know much about.

What I did have on my side was a lot of bygone performer friends who had delved into real estate after their professional entertainment days were done. And having heard story after story from them about how competitive the real estate industry was and how they felt as if they were "shouting into the void" whenever they posted anything on social media, I saw my opening.

I quickly started asking my real estate friends if I could run ads for them to help generate buyer and seller leads. They agreed, and I discovered that I was moderately good at creating these types of ads. Word spread as they told their real estate pals, and *voila*, my first baby business was born.

Now, I say "baby business," but in reality, I felt like I had hit the big time with real estate marketing. I made six figures in my first nine months and attracted the attention of a seven-figure company that asked me to step in as the CEO of their new real estate marketing division.

This is it! I made it! I thought. And I had. I had successfully reinvented myself. I had learned how to capitalize on a whole new skill set that I didn't even realize I had. And I had taken myself from unemployed opera singer to rockstar CEO in a matter of months.

But even beyond all of that, I had done the ONE thing that set me up for discovering my Million Dollar Identity. I couldn't have known it at the time, but I had put myself on a trajectory to cashing in on being the number one authority in my niche—a niche that just happens to be a billion-dollar industry.

All the stars seemed to be aligning once again. Real estate marketing had put me back in the driver's seat of my rocket ship to reclaim my dream life. Business was going great. I had just signed a huge contract with a new company. What could possibly go wrong?

Enter COVID-19.

Paused. Paused. Paused. Canceled. One by one, the phone rang with my clients calling to share the unpleasant news that they were pausing their campaigns. Again, I sat in disbelief as I listened to the world collectively gasp and then shut down (or endlessly debate about whether to shut down).

Do you know what is not good for a brand new baby business? Economic uncertainty. And the pandemic had served us up a heaping helping of economic uncertainty.

Not again, I thought. *Could a person really crash and burn twice within the span of two years?* The answer is "yes," of course, but I was determined not to let it happen to me. Instead of feeling sorry for myself, I decided this time wouldn't be like the last time.

I wasn't going to allow myself to be defeated and fall back into panic mode. This time, I would keep my head. So, I started viewing the situation objectively rather than letting my emotions take charge.

That's when I asked myself the key question that I regularly ask my clients:

What do you WILL?

I remembered that when I was singing in Europe, the way I became a #1 hit bestselling artist was by getting my music into top publications and on podcasts, which helped establish me as a credible singer in Europe. In other words, I willed it through my actions. I figured I could take those same skills and apply them to real estate. And that's just what I did.

By looking at what I had and asking that simple question, "What do I *will?*" I saw the way forward. I willed myself into becoming the #1 nationally recognized real estate marketer through a public relations blitz campaign.

The results exceeded my wildest expectations. Within 30 days, not only had I gotten published on top real estate blogs and been a guest on high-ranking podcasts, but I even managed to land a contributorship in the #1 real estate publication in the world, *Inman News*.

And here's the icing on the cake. After they invited me to be a contributor, they asked me to speak on their virtual stage during an international conference being broadcast to over 1,000 realtors. It's true what they say: you only need 1,000 loyal fans to be successful, and I was well on my way to developing my fan base.

During that first month of the pandemic, I went from having 80 percent of my clients either pause or cancel their marketing projects to building my client base beyond my previous capacity.

That's right. In a time when no one was getting clients, I found myself needing to hire employees to help me serve my growing client base. My marketing friends took notice and asked me if I could do what I was doing in my niche for their niches.

This was my "aha" moment.

Talking to journalists and pitching editors came as easily to me as singing or breathing. I knew how to craft a story because I'd been doing it my whole life. I had built my career as an opera singer through grassroots, organic, earned media publicity, and now I was ready to transfer that knowledge to a new niche.

Within three months, I made over six figures in my newfound PR business. That's when I knew I was onto something, and not just financially. I had found my passion.

I was no longer a former professional opera singer. I was the CEO of Victorious PR, and I loved that feeling! Starting my PR firm gave me the power to rewrite my story.

Having once lived my life in the spotlight, I was excited to have the opportunity to shine the spotlight on others. Discovering my passion for PR and realizing the value that others saw in the work I was doing made me feel right at home for the first time since my visa had been denied.

When your passion and skills collide with an empowering story, it blows the lid off of your success.

Within our first year of business, Victorious PR reached over $1 million in revenue. And so far, in our second year, we've already passed the $3 million mark with no sign of slowing down.

So what's our secret?

It's pretty simple. We truly "talk our talk" and "walk our walk."

Our business grew organically through PR efforts alone. We didn't run any paid ads during the first 12 months. Instead, we gained authority and credibility steadily by putting in the work. This is how I'm able to confidently offer PR services to my clients; I use the exact same systems and techniques for them that I used to grow my own business.

We focus on finding specific story angles and niche media markets where we know each client can shine, and we beat out the competition.

I want you to ask yourself this one question: *If I were to start a business tomorrow, how would I gain the respect of those outside of my current network?* Sure, your current network can help you start your next big thing, but to see this type of growth and launch your rocket to success, you need to establish yourself as THE go-to authority in your niche.

The first step must be building your own personal brand. Ask yourself, *How will I stand out?* It is vitally important that your digital footprint is one of credibility and authority.

We live in a world of disconnect, misinformation, miscommunication, and fake news. Figuring out who we can trust is no longer a matter of looking someone in the eye and getting a firm handshake. It takes more effort to earn the trust of high-level clients.

It's always important to take an honest look at where you are before you can begin constructing the bridge to your beautiful, dreamy future. I want you to consider your own situation and ask yourself the question I asked myself before I started Victorious PR:

What Do I Will?

Instead of focusing on what you don't have, I want you to really think about what you *do* have. Then think about what you have the will-power to create with those skills and tools.

I want you to close your eyes and really paint the picture for yourself. Don't be afraid to get too detailed here. What does it feel like to stand on top of your mountain? What do you see, touch, taste, and smell every day?

Maybe it's a high-rise office view overlooking the city. Maybe you can smell that glorious new car smell as you drive around in your brand new Tesla and taste the champagne as you toast to your first six-figure month.

Whatever you imagine, I want you to spend some time—even just five minutes—each day thinking about that dream vision.

Next, I want you to consider how PR can help you achieve your goals. In fact, I'd argue that PR can be the bridge between your current situation and your beautiful dreamy future because here's a hard truth: there can only be ONE #1 authority in any niche.

Is that you, or is it your competitor? If I do a Google search for your niche, who's going to pop up? Who's going to take first place? If it's not you, then you're behind. In this day and age, there's only one person who gets to be "King" or "Queen." And the good news is that you have the power to make sure it's you.

I am living proof of the power of PR.

Prior to three years ago, no one outside of the opera-singing world knew the name Victoria Kennedy.

Through my own experience building two businesses, I also realized how critical personal branding is. When I started down the real estate marketing path, establishing my credibility and authority early on gave me the platform I needed to then turn around and build a thriving PR business.

This is where I see CEOs and business owners stumble the most—failing to recognize how important their brand name truly is to the success of their business.

And to be fair, I didn't recognize how important building my personal brand was at first either. It's hard to see when you're deep in it, putting out fires and focusing on putting one foot in front of another.

At the time, I didn't realize how much I learned working hard for that first year in real estate marketing, proving my worth, experimenting to figure out how to get editors to notice me, and showing people that I was credible by getting into the top real estate publications.

All of that experience gave me the foundation to immediately build a million-dollar business from scratch. And when I look back on the whirlwind adventure I've been on, I can see clearly how everything worked in my favor. The publications, podcasts, and speaking engagements established me as an authority, which is why I believe so strongly in personal branding and using PR to develop that credibility in your niche.

Premium, quality PR is not just about getting into top publications. It's about figuring out how to tell your unique story. It's about taking your audience along on a journey with you and letting them see how you build your credibility. It's about starting small and telling a story with your brand.

Think about what would impress your audience more … Seeing you in that #1 in your industry leader spot or hearing your personal story about how you rose from the ashes to claim that #1 industry leader spot?

Everyone loves a good underdog story, especially if you can make them feel like they've played a part in your success. So getting you into top publications only scratches the surface of what a custom PR strategy can do for you.

Make sure to tell the story your audience needs to hear. And then focus on telling that story by getting your articles featured in publications that your audience actually cares about. For example, when I was in real estate, it wasn't enough to get into a publication like *Forbes*. Real estate agents don't care about *Forbes*; they care about the #1 real estate publication in the world. Once my article was featured there, I was invited to speak at a conference sponsored by the same publication, and that's when the stars aligned perfectly.

That is how you become the #1 authority in your field. That is how you rise up and take your place as the Industry Leader. Consider what your audience is listening to, what they're reading, and what they're watching. Then, use the power of PR to position yourself as the industry leader in your specific niche.

If you're looking to build your own Million Dollar Identity, book a call with Victorious PR so that we can help you score the credibility and authority you deserve:

Go.VictoriousPR.com

CHAPTER THREE

DAN ASHBURN

Dan Ashburn

Dan Ashburn began his career in the digital space when he was barely old enough to attend primary school. His tenacity, hunger for knowledge, and entrepreneurial drive led him to start multiple businesses. Dan currently holds equity in several million-dollar brands. His business, Titan Network, has 1,000+ Amazon sellers who contribute to its progression with the latest training, strategy, tools, and tactics in the market.

TRUST YOUR INSTINCTS

It's 1996, I'm around seven years old, and I'm excited to hear the chime of Windows 95 as our first home computer switches on. My mom teaches me to open Microsoft Word and the basics of typing. And I can't wait for the dial-up tone of our new 56k modem to finish connecting.

It connects, and this whole new world opens up to me. I spend every minute of every day diving deeper and deeper into the emerging world of the internet. Then, my Dad asks me to type up his 30,000+ word company documentation. I can't wait.

Two years later, the inevitable millennium bug—Y2K—is almost here, and I just have to solve it.

I learned how to reset the clock and apply the patch. I was nine when I found myself updating 30+ computers at my dad's company. Hours of research, making real-life updates; it felt amazing!

I was hooked on computers and the web. It just made sense to me.

Soon after, I started my first company, Web Spider Limited (in my dad's name, of course). I built basic websites in Macromedia Dreamweaver and then Yahoo! Geocities for my dad's company and many of his friends. Meanwhile, I discovered the world of making money online and fell in love with Search Engine Optimization.

Then, my world flipped upside down.

My parents divorced when I was twelve, and my mom moved us to Tenerife, Canary Islands, Spain, with her new partner.

My early teens were turbulent. Navigating family troubles, being one of the only English kids in a Spanish village, unsuccessfully avoiding the temptation of island party life, and attempting to get through school, I was heading down the wrong path.

Nevertheless, I spent hours exploring online business models, learning web development, SEO, and affiliate marketing. I became known as the kid who could "fix your internet" or "build your website."

Partying on weekends, doing school during the day, and spending every other waking minute until the early hours on sites like ClickBank, Warrior Forum, and SEO Moz, I would make money, lose money, and get lost for days, mastering how to rank websites in Google.

I was obsessed.

By 2005, I was almost 16, and the Tenerife environment had gotten the better of me, so I was "sent" back to the UK to live with my dad. He wasn't a big fan of me living with him. He said he could put me up in his rental property just down the road from the local college, but I had to cover the bills.

This was my chance.

I somehow got into the local college based on the two GCSEs (General Certificate of Secondary Education) that I had managed to get while in Tenerife and the two courses I took in Computing and Business Studies.

The following year was a haze, full of drinking, drugs, and being an all-around idiot.

Something had to change.

To make ends meet, I worked in a local bar in the evenings and maintained a small number of websites for local businesses. I woke up one morning, still hungover from the night before, and heard an advert on the radio, "The Royal Air Force is looking for talented IT personnel."

I can do that.

So I got up, typed my application letter, and got on the train to the Military Careers Office.

Six weeks later, I was in basic training.

Everyone around me, including my closest family, told me it was a stupid idea.

"You will never make it."

"You will quit."

I knew deep down that I had what it takes.

Ten weeks later, I completed basic training and earned commendations along the way, including being a course leader for my intake. Next was twelve months of technical training at No. 1 Radio School, RAF Cosford.

Even though I found myself in trouble at times, I graduated without setbacks, and I set a new record for getting 100% on the Cisco exam and gaining Microsoft qualifications. I was posted to RAF Coningsby in the UK, where I met my Sergeant, Charlie; Corporal, Paul; and Flight Lieutenant, Brad.

I quickly found myself outpacing my peers but struggling with the bureaucracy of rank. I would be told to "work within my rank" and "that's not how we do it." It made no sense to me.

Progression was based on your time in a post or the luck of the draw on where you were posted, rather than skill or talent and ability to contribute. Luckily, I found myself on a particular project that had me working closely with my seniors, who by this point were managing me to my strengths and accommodating my weaknesses in abiding by the "norm."

I was freelancing on web design, running a web hosting company, getting bigger and better at affiliate marketing, and flipping websites on sites such as Flippa.com to earn extra cash on the side.

One day, Charlie pulled me into his office and proposed that I pursue becoming a commissioned officer. He gave me the career advice I needed to qualify and sent me off.

That was it. I was going to be an officer.

But I doubted myself. *Was I really a leader?*

Brad fully supported me and coached me in private on what I needed to do, and I worked toward it.

Twelve months later, I'd just gotten back from a tour in the Middle East, where I continued to do freelance work from a bunker! While there, I called my best friend John back home. He worked as a call center manager, barely making ends meet, but had the work ethic of a stallion. I told him to call the accountant and to trust me because we were starting a company together.

Webfold was born.

Shortly after, Brad pulled me into his office and gave me the confirmation I needed and had been feeling for a while.

"You need to follow your dreams," he said.

He acknowledged that while my contribution to the country would be significant, my contribution to the world could be much more if I leaned into my desires. That was the permission I needed.

So, with the full support of my girlfriend, Lotty (who would later become my wife), I wrote a letter of acceptance to a new job as the CEO of Webfold and fast-tracked my way out of the military.

This was the scariest, most exciting thing I had ever done, and I had nothing to lose.

Working from the back bedroom of my two-bedroom flat with a £50-per-week budget, sharing a mattress on the floor with my girlfriend, I was ready to take on the world. And the next day, John decided he was going to quit his job, too.

We spent every hour of every day working the phones, emailing prospective clients, and reaching the point of leading a local BNI chapter.

We went from my back bedroom to my mother-in-law's garage to a floor of offices and 30+ staff in the center of Birmingham. We quickly built a seven-figure business on blood, sweat, and tears.

And we went on to build hundreds of websites, deploy hundreds of successful SEO campaigns, and help many local businesses thrive. I had made a name for myself in the SEO space as "the kid that is really good at SEO."

I'd worked with a local jeweler to sell bullion online through a hacked Magento website while running SEO and PPC on a shoestring budget. We hit over $2 million a month in sales and became one of the top three bullion suppliers in the UK. (I recently heard from the owner, confirming that the website made $100,000,000 in 2020!)

Meanwhile, the Google Slap happened.

Google changed the way SEO works forever, and many companies died overnight. They were penalized for past activity, and their websites were wiped off the face of the earth.

I had to help.

I tested repeatedly and became really good at recovering websites from the penalty and getting them back to the top of Google. Because of this, I was introduced to Sandeep, an up-and-coming authority in cosmetic dentistry in the UK.

Sandeep wanted more patients.

John and I tested everything and mastered patient generation. We were producing results no one else had seen in the market for a specific product, Invisalign, and Sandeep wanted to go all in. We opened the UK's first Invisalign and built the UK's largest Invisalign provider, MiSmile.

This was the hardest thing I had ever committed to. I was stressed, and I doubted our ability.

We had over 50 dental practices in the network relying on us to make thousands of pounds of Invisalign cases show up. There was no hiding behind impressions or brand awareness.

We had to make money show up with a tight budget across 50 geographic locations in the UK with different populations and demographics.

These were some of the most stressful times of my life, but I knew we could do it, and we did. Working for myself, with a good team, a great partner, offices, and a loving and supportive wife … the works.

I was living the dream … Right?

Wrong. I was miserable.

What I thought was the dream turned out to be a living hell, being glued to my desk 18+ hours a day. I was a slave to my business, constantly pursuing the next big idea.

I created Hello Taxi before Uber went private in the UK and wiped us out.

I created a tradesperson directory before Rated People and others emerged.

For one reason or another, all had great potential but never quite made it. And I had dragged Lotty on that roller coaster with no end in sight. Then one afternoon in early 2014, I received an email.

"Make $10,000 per month selling on Amazon."

It felt real to me. Something tangible, worth real money that wasn't tied to any location or client. And I didn't know you could sell on Amazon at the time unless you were a "big brand," but I dived in.

I took the fast track by copying someone who had already achieved the same result I wanted to achieve. I quickly convinced John to spend the dwindling profit we had in the bank on this program and took the course. And I told Lotty, "This is it!"

A month later, I was on a plane to an event in Las Vegas.

I was terrified.

What are these people going to think of me?

All this self-doubt was creeping in. I decided to do what I know best— help people using the only thing I am good at.

I quickly found myself at the heart of the community, surrounded by amazing people who believed in and inspired me. Half of Webfold had become Dominate Dental, and the other half focused on Amazon.

We were set.

We were going to make millions of dollars on Amazon! We launched our first product, puppy pee mats, and the first sales came in while we slept.

WTF!

This actually works.

But it wasn't off into the sunset from there. Twelve months later, we were doing okay but at a frustratingly slow pace. We were split among servicing our old clients, helping dentists, growing our brand, and helping others with theirs.

There weren't many in the community back then who had the internet marketing experience to apply to Amazon. We helped people with their brand websites, content, and ranking on Amazon (back in the old days of press releases, etc.). And I developed connections and friends in the Amazon world.

But our split focus was killing us.

Again, something had to change.

At the same time, Sandeep had offered me a full-time director role in MiSmile with a six-figure salary and options. But on one condition … I stop everything else and give it my all.

This meant more stability and guaranteed money than I had ever had. I saw myself being set for life, but something didn't feel right. I was already struggling with the corporate structure, not working on something that was truly mine.

It took three months to make one of the most complex decisions of my life. I decided to go all-in on Amazon, and John decided to step back and focus exclusively on Dominate. It worked. The effect on momentum and success was instant.

Once Amazon became my 100% focus, the network I'd been developing in that world for the last year began to open doors. In fact, one of my closest friends in the Amazon world was Kirsty.

Kirsty ran a small coaching business alongside her Amazon business, helping other sellers. She'd been introduced to another friend called Scott, who had a big vision. They needed someone to handle the tactical leadership, so Kirsty brought me in.

All the self-doubt came back. *Can I do this? Am I really good enough? Who am I to tell people I can grow these brands?*

We started working together, merging my Amazon team, Kirsty's Amazon coaching business, and Scott's consulting business. We wrote a course called "Build Scale Exit," and I knew we needed promotion partners to promote it.

This is where I met Athena. Athena was an influencer in the community, connecting people and hosting events.

I approached Athena on promoting the course, and Athena, being Athena, flipped it and had me go out to China to mentor her on her trip, China Magic. At the time, I was still the guy in the background. And I suddenly understood the meaning of imposter syndrome.

I was shaking.

But I did it.

Scott and I went to China to mentor 50 sellers on Amazon. I found myself becoming a partner and co-creator from the third trip onward. Athena and I made six more trips before the pandemic hit.

What I hadn't realized was that I was now on two paths.

I tried to make the two worlds work together. Make everyone align. But the vision among us—Kirsty, Scott, and me—was breaking down. We realized we had likely made the wrong decision to combine three business models into one.

We decided to split them out, and I was given an ultimatum: strategic consulting (and rolling up brands) or coaching. I chose the option that felt most natural to me: helping people succeed on Amazon.

I loved it.

I was experiencing real purpose and tangible impact, holding others accountable to become the best they could be. I was leading.

It hit home when my father-in-law, Charles, asked me to talk to a colleague at the BBC who wanted to get out of the 9–5 and had heard what I was doing on Amazon. He was miserable in his role as a producer, and Charles convinced me to talk to him. (I had to do it because there was a seriously good bowl of curry in it for me!)

His name was Phil. I went on to coach him over WhatsApp and helped point him in the right direction.

Just five years prior, Phil was a producer on the BBC. Today, Phil sold his first brand of multi-seven figures and was already at the point of selling his second for a lot more. A multi-millionaire, Phil travels the world with his beautiful girlfriend, living life to its full potential. *And I was a part of making that happen.*

Around this time, though, China Magic was becoming an issue. I couldn't get everyone to align. I had to make a choice.

But I was scared.

I buried my head.

While on my fourth China Magic trip, Athena and I sat down and realized how much impact China Magic had in 12 days and asked ourselves, *How can we make this happen all year?* And that's when we got the idea for Titan Network.

We stayed up until 2:00 a.m. writing a letter to our attendees that they would wake up to. And just like that, we had the first 50 members.

Titan Network, the exclusive membership organization for elite Amazon sellers, was born.

Athena and I continued to build Titan Network. Titan Network is not about Athena or me or any of our 40+ leaders and mentors. It's about the combined power of all of us with a shared vision, knowing that together we are stronger—experience handed down in the purest form.

I also got to know a guy named Rich Henderson quite well through all of the trips to Vegas. Rich approached me with the idea to join Amazing.com and co-create Amazing Selling Machine.

30,000+ members. The original community that created our industry.

This was a proud and defining point for me ... but also the scariest yet. I was close to saying no. But I thought back to how I had gotten to where I was.

I decided to lean into the fear.

Skip ahead to today, and I hold equity in multiple million-dollar brands and operate at the highest level in the industry. Titan Network has 1,000+ Amazon sellers who contribute to its progress with the latest training, strategies, tools, and tactics in the market.

We are at the leading edge of selling on Amazon, underpinned by a culture and community that is hard to believe until you experience it. We run events worldwide multiple times a year and are really building something special.

Meanwhile, I've been raising two beautiful children with my wife, Lotty, showing them every day what is possible in this world when you believe in yourself and know what you want.

When I reflect on my journey and pinpoint the one thing that got me to where I am, *it's trust.*

Trust in yourself.

Trust in your intuition.

Trust in the thing that gives you purpose.

If it feels right, it usually is. If it feels wrong, it usually is. How quickly you listen to how it feels and act upon it ultimately determines how fast you achieve it.

If you believe you can, you will.

When you're scared shitless, shaking with crippling anxiety and stress, you're outside your comfort zone—*that's where you grow.* That's where you level up.

There are many points in my journey where this was true:

- On the wrong track, switching to the military

- Quitting the military and my career to pursue my dream as an entrepreneur

- Stepping up to a higher level and producing for Invisalign

- Getting on the plane to Vegas to learn about Amazon

- Saying Yes to Kirsty and stepping up to the challenge

- Saying Yes to Athena and stepping up to the challenge

- Saying Yes to Amazing and stepping up to the challenge

- Starting Titan Network and stepping up to the challenge

All terrifying.

All exciting.

All new levels of growth.

You know what you need to do. No one is going to do it for you. You have an idea of where you see yourself in the future. Get real clear on it *and go after it.*

How fast and how successfully you get there comes down to your ability to listen to your intuition. So, take action on it and surround yourself with like-minded people and loved ones who believe in you more than you do. People that have already done what you're looking to achieve.

It's the founding principle of what Titan Network is built on.

And I invite you to be a part of it, too, at:

TitanNetwork.com

CHAPTER FOUR

KIANA DANIAL

Kiana Danial

Kiana Danial, CEO at Invest Diva, is an award-winning *Wall Street Journal* and *USA Today* bestselling author. An internationally recognized personal-investing expert, she has been featured in publications such as *The Wall Street Journal, TIME, Forbes, Kiplinger, Business Insider, TheStreet, Nasdaq,* and has appeared on *Fox Business, CNNi, Yahoo! Finance,* and *Cheddar* to share her expertise.

Kiana is a highly sought-after commentator, professional speaker, and executive coach who has reported on the financial markets directly from the floor of the NYSE and NASDAQ. Using her Diva Wealth Ecosystem, she built a $7M net worth within three years.

A six-time author, Kiana's books include the WSJ bestseller, *Million Dollar Family Secrets: Make Your Money Work for You to Create Generational Wealth,* and the bestselling *Cryptocurrency Investing for Dummies,* published by Wiley in 2019. She also won the Two Comma Club Award from ClickFunnels in 2021.

Kiana's mission with the Invest Diva movement is to empower and educate moms to take control of their financial future by investing in the online financial markets and building a wealth ecosystem.

BUILD YOUR MILLIONAIRE DIVA WEALTH ECOSYSTEM

It was a year after I had left Tokyo for New York City, and it felt like I finally had it all: a dream job on Wall Street, a boyfriend, and an apartment on the Upper East Side—just like what I had seen in the movies and on TV in shows like *Gossip Girl*, *Sex and the City*, and *Friends*.

It was 2011, and I was living the life of my dreams. But little did I know, things were about to change.

On a day I thought I had achieved an amazing performance, I got fired.

A few days later, my boyfriend dumped me.

Soon after, I ran out of money to pay rent.

It wasn't the first time I had hit rock bottom through my journey from Iran to Japan to the United States. But it felt like the worst one.

I had always thought that by the time I turned 27, I would have everything figured out.

I had finally tasted what it felt like to have it all … and BAM. Just like that, it was all taken away from me.

What are my parents going to think? What are people going to say? Where am I going to live? What if no one will ever love me? I felt like a failure. Again.

I suddenly realized I was falling into an old habit—the old habit that had me falling down to rock bottom time and time again.

The one that was driving me into a welfare house. It was my ...

Welfare Diva Mentality.

While I was trying to blame my misfortune—my drop from the top to the bottom—on external factors such as "bad luck," a "horrible boss," or a "lousy boyfriend," the real reason could only be found within ME. I had fallen back into the pattern I inherited from generations before me. That is why every time I've come into big money and happiness, it's been short-lived, and I've lost it.

We see this over and over again with lottery winners. Seventy percent of them LOSE all of their money and end up bankrupt just a few years after receiving a large payout. Why is that?

The vast majority of people simply don't have the internal capacity to create and hold onto large amounts of money. They are not prepared to face the increased challenges that go with more money and success.

It suddenly became clear to me: I had fallen down to rock bottom—yet again—because deep down I didn't think I deserved the "Upper East Side" luxury living.

It was time to snap out of it forever. It was time to become a ...

Millionaire Diva.

The first step on this journey to becoming a millionaire and having financial freedom (which was my goal) was to get rid of my old beliefs about money.

Changing this one belief was a huge "aha" moment in my transformation. Money doesn't make you a good or a bad person. All it does is amplify who you truly are.

If someone is inherently stingy, mean, or ill-spirited, having more money will simply amplify those traits. If they're helpful, generous, considerate, charitable, and positive, becoming a millionaire will echo their good vibes. Money is a tool that magnifies what's already there.

By becoming a millionaire, you can become the change you've always wanted to see in the world.

That was so liberating for me!

I told myself: *Enough is enough. I'm going to take things into my own hands.* I needed to change both my mindset and my strategies to obtain my goal of becoming financially free.

I became obsessed with learning about finance and wealth. I started interning for free in small financial firms to learn different investing strategies. I studied for the CFP and CMT and CFA—all these fancy certified financial titles the money managers had.

I went through the courses, gleaning all the knowledge, but I didn't actually take the final exams to become certified. If I had, then I would have had to follow their regulations. That would have restricted me from educating people on social media venues, and my goal is to educate people to become their own CFPs.

I also started investing on my own and documented my trading journey in my first book, which ended up getting published by McGraw-Hill.

Investing is the best thing you can do with your money. But you may be thinking, *Ok, well where do I even start?*

Do I have to go create a bunch of accounts and invest in a bunch of opportunities and hope for them to turn into more money? Should I respond to the DM I just got on Instagram from this person claiming they made a bunch of money with a broker and trying to "hook me up"?

The short answer is no. And please, do not EVER hand your money to someone who slides in your DM without first actually verifying they are legit.

Social media impersonators and fake accounts are the number one reason why people get scammed in the financial industry.

Unfortunately, there is another dark side to today's financial industry, and that is the professional scamming business. If you follow me on any of my social media accounts—Instagram, Facebook, TikTok, or Twitter—you'll soon start getting messages and followers from someone who looks like me, has a variation of my name or Invest Diva, pretends to be me, and asks you to give them money.

This happens to almost all other legitimate financial institutions and educators. So I'm here to show you how to avoid these by following the right path to making your money work for you.

The first thing you need to do when starting your investing journey is to create an account with a broker or an exchange so that you can get access to the online financial markets.

What Is a Broker?

It's never been easier to invest in online financial assets thanks to the advent of the internet and online brokers. An online brokerage allows you to access the financial markets and participate in the buying and selling of financial instruments like stocks. Online brokers are the intermediary between buyers and sellers. They facilitate the purchase and sale of financial assets in an online environment and typically make money by charging the investors a commission fee or by adding a markup to the stock price.

There are online brokers in almost all countries. Regardless of where you are, you should be able to invest, but make sure that you're selecting a credible broker.

Depending on the asset type you're planning to invest in (i.e., stocks, cryptocurrency, or forex) you may need to find a specialized broker or exchange.

Choosing a Stock Brokerage

Choosing a broker, just like anything else in personal finance, is personal. You need to find a broker that suits your needs. At Invest Diva, we encourage investors to participate in "Value Investing." This means buying an asset and holding it for the long term to maximize gains. In that case, you wouldn't need the highly advanced brokerage accounts that are mainly used by large hedge funds and day traders, which can also save you a ton of money on commission fees.

As more people become interested in investing on their own, many online brokers have adopted the passive investing style, and many even forgo the commission fee charged on your transactions because you are parking your money in their brokerage long term.

The most important things to remember before choosing a broker are the level of regulation, trust, and insurance. Here's the checklist of things to look for in the terms or disclaimer portion of their website. You can also research the brokerage on the SIPC website.

1. Your brokerage must be a member of the Financial Industry Regulatory Authority (FINRA).

2. Your brokerage must be covered by the Federal Deposit Insurance Corporation (FDIC).

3. Your brokerage must carry insurance with a per-customer limit of at least $500,000, with $250,000 available for cash claims. If you're looking to invest more than this amount, then you need to either diversify among a number of brokers or call your broker and ask for increased insurance.

4. Your brokerage should also be willing to reimburse you for losses resulting from fraud. Make sure you double-check what the brokerage requires of you in order for you to be reimbursed. Find out if you have to provide any documentation or take specific precautions to protect yourself.

Here are some brokerages for stocks in the US, UK, European Union, Australia, and Canada that either myself or our Invest Diva students have used with an acceptable level of satisfaction:

🇺🇸	TD Ameritrade, Interactive Brokers, Charles Schwab, Public, Webull, Fidelity, E-Trade
🇬🇧🇪🇺	SaxoBank, Degiro
🇦🇺	CMC, Self Wealth, Interactive Brokers
🇨🇦	Questrade, Interactive Brokers

Almost all of the above brokerages facilitate investing in all international and US stocks, as well as Index Funds. If you're looking to diversify outside of the stock market and into assets such as cryptocurrency, then you need to find a specialized exchange or broker that can facilitate cryptocurrency investments.

Choosing a Cryptocurrency Exchange

The most popular way to buy cryptocurrencies, though, is to go directly through an online cryptocurrency exchange. However, depending on your cryptocurrency investing goals, you may need to consider alternative methods. For example, if you're an active crypto trader, you may find a traditional cryptocurrency exchange or a broker easier to use. But if you just want to buy some cryptos and park them in your wallet, a trusted online/local exchange can do the job. In this chapter, I tell you all about different types of exchanges, brokers, and other cryptocurrency providers and show you how to choose the right one(s) for your cryptocurrency goals.

The most popular types of cryptocurrency exchanges are called *Centralized Exchanges*. Centralized exchanges are like traditional stock exchanges. The buyers and sellers come together, and the exchange plays the role of a middleman. These exchanges typically charge a commission to facilitate the transactions made between buyers and sellers.

Here's how a centralized exchange typically works:

1. You give your money to the exchange.

2. The exchange holds it for you (like a bank or a trusted middleman).

3. You watch the prices of the available cryptocurrencies on the exchange.

4. Depending on the exchange, you can trade your fiat currency (a traditional currency, like the US dollar) for a cryptocurrency (like Bitcoin). With most exchanges, however, you will find better luck exchanging two cryptocurrencies for one another.

5. You place your order.

6. The exchange finds a seller to match your buy order. If you're selling, the exchange finds you a buyer.

7. Tada! You just crypto shopped on an exchange.

In my book, *Cryptocurrency Investing For Dummies* (published by Wiley, 2019), I go into further detail about choosing crypto exchanges and the best investing practices that are beyond the scope of this book.

Some of my favorite cryptocurrency exchanges in the US include Coinbase, Gemini, and Kraken.

Recently, stockbrokers such as Robinhood have also enabled cryptocurrency trading features, but there's a big catch. One of the biggest reasons people invest in cryptocurrency is to buy and hold long-term to maximize capital gains. Please note that if you invest in cryptocurrencies through a broker such as Robinhood, you will not actually own the cryptocurrency. You will simply be taking a position on its price.

Please promise me that you won't invest in cryptocurrency before actually understanding how it works. To find out if it actually suits your risk tolerance, go through the *Seven Deadly Mistakes Crypto Investors Make (And How to Avoid Them)* on **CryptoMistakes.com**.

Pro Tip: Once you choose your broker, always make sure you activate the Two-Factor Authentication (2FA) on your platform. Two-factor authentication is a method of confirming your claimed identity by using a combination of two different factors: something the exchange knows (like your password) and something it has (like a six-digit number it sends to your mobile phone or your email address for the second step of the verification).

I was now an expert with my personal investing and a published author, I was becoming a recognized expert in the investing world, and my portfolio was increasing through my investment and compounding strategies. My ecosystem had many elements of what could turn me into a Millionaire Diva fast … but it was still missing one very important ingredient.

If I had had this ONE key ingredient ten years ago when I first started my Invest Diva journey, I would probably be on my private island in Bora Bora right now. Which legit makes me angry!

So what was this missing element in my Diva Wealth Ecosystem?

The missing element that I needed to complete my Diva Wealth Ecosystem was an offer. I needed to figure out how to turn my passion and expertise into an offer that creates value for others. I always knew I wanted to help more people take control of their financial future. I was passionate about helping women in male-dominated fields. I knew it was especially important for moms to start investing for their children from the moment they are born in order to set them up financially.

I then decided to help more people who were intimidated by the whole financial world and founded the Invest Diva Movement and learn.investdiva.com to help thousands of people take control of their financial future.

A millionaire in our day and age lives a similar life to a middle-class corporate manager in the '70s. Millionaire status shouldn't feel outside your reach. If you want the ease that comes with having more than enough, then it's important that you aspire to become a millionaire.

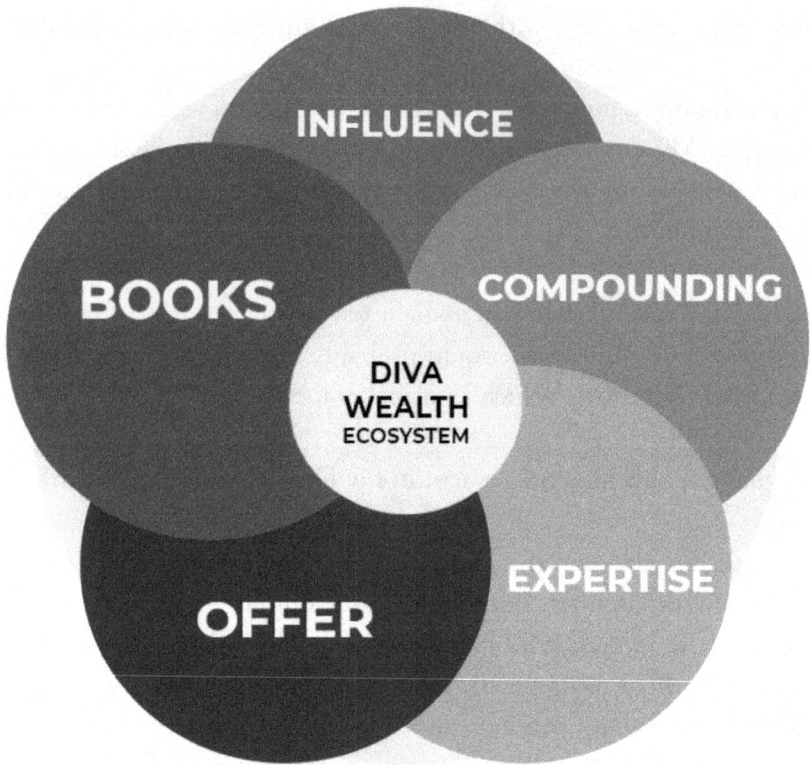

You need to set financial goals so you can create a strategy to actually achieve them.

You need to have a specific plan with a feasible deadline that feels achievable to you. Once you get to your first goal, then you can move on to the next level. I went from a $50K goal to a $100K goal, then to $200K, and then on to a $1 million goal. Now that I have my Diva Wealth Ecosystem in place, my portfolio is on track to grow to $100 million in the next five years.

You need to write down why you are investing so you will be able to choose the right assets for your unique goals and financial situation. The answer normally falls into one or more of the following options:

- Income
- Retirement
- Generational wealth

In my opinion, generational wealth is the best reason to start investing. It has become the core of our education at Invest Diva. We achieve this investing through a framework called the Zen Wealth Generator. In simplistic terms, if you do these three things, you're going to get to the next level: invest in yourself, increase your income, and invest in financial assets to make your money work for you.

When you combine all three steps, things can move at a FAST pace without having to take too much risk.

Completing my Diva Wealth Ecosystem has been a blessing, allowing me to work because I want to, not because I have to. I can now sleep with less stress and anxiety around money. I can order food without looking at the price on the menu. I can tip more for services. I can set up a foundation to help support the causes I care about.

Having a Diva Wealth Ecosystem enables us to support the causes that are important to our community. Every year, we take a poll from our students to discover their favorite charities, and we contribute to them on behalf of the Invest Diva Movement.

Of course, the money is great. But what is even greater is the profound impact we've been able to make, changing thousands of lives around the world. That's a side effect I didn't foresee.

Thanks to the simple decision I made to create an offer that creates value for others, our students have paid off student debt and mortgages, adopted children, sent their kids to college, paid for health care, started businesses, and even quit their jobs. Some (like my husband and I) are contemplating early retirement, discussing having another baby, or considering moving to their favorite destinations (ours is Hawaii). They're fulfilling their dreams.

Seeing all the results we've been able to create for our students has been far more rewarding than the income alone. Our *Make Your Money Work For You PowerCourse* now has over 3,000 students who share their Diva Wins and Divo Wins on a daily basis.

As I have achieved financial freedom and don't ever have to work again, you may be asking, "Why are you still working?"

The answer is simple: to help others.

Once you achieve everything you've ever dreamed of in life and have made sure your family is set up financially, you become addicted to sharing your journey and helping others achieve the same results.

I've seen how many people read my books, watch my educational social media videos, and even take my free classes. They get excited, feel empowered, and feel confident they can do it, and then they get in and they get frustrated, stuck, and consider giving up.

They're so close to getting to the next level. But they're so frustrated with little tactics that they forget about the process and give the whole thing up.

It breaks my heart because I know I can help them, so personally, my goal is to help one million moms take control of their financial future by the year 2025.

And that's why we're rapidly expanding our team to work closely with students who are ready to use the power of the Zen Wealth Generator to create generational wealth. We call it the Invest Diva Movement.

If you're serious (not just curious) about increasing your income, I'd like to invite you to sign up for my free "Make Your Money Work for You Masterclass." This is my #1 most popular training that teaches busy individuals how to take control of their financial future—even if they've never invested before, suck at math, or don't have a ton of money.

Over 150K people have signed up for this masterclass, and my students are people from all walks of life: single moms, burnt-out nurses, doctors, lawyers, engineers and entrepreneurs who, following my process, have grown their portfolio to over $200K, $500K and even $1M.

I know some people might be thinking they need to have a big chunk of money to start investing, but I actually recommend people start small. For example, if you're a parent, and you start investing just $50/month for your kids the moment they are born, they will hit the million-dollar status by the time they retire.

The best time to start investing was 20 years ago, but the second-best time to start is now—especially with a recession that could be headed our way.

My superpower is breaking down complicated financial strategies into an easy-to-understand roadmap so that anyone can build significant wealth through investing, even if they don't have a lot of time or are bad at math. You can sign up for my free masterclass by going to:

Learn.InvestDiva.com

CHAPTER FIVE

ERIC BEER

Eric Beer

Eric Beer is the founder and CEO of Universal Marketing Partners (UMP), Performance Marketer™, and the SaaS survey software SurveyDetective™. He has been using survey and quiz strategies to generate over 50 million leads for businesses since 2003. Eric has scaled multiple online businesses to nine figures and has generated millions in revenue for himself and his clients using his expertise in performance marketing.

In 2019, Eric launched the *Performance Marketer* podcast to share his online marketing expertise and make an impact in the lives of other entrepreneurs. Eric and his brilliant and beautiful wife Allison live in New York with their two remarkable children, Ashley and Zachary, and a dog named Ozzy.

START A DIALOGUE,
NOT A MONOLOGUE

When the company I worked for went out of business, more than 300 people got laid off—including me. At the time, my wife and I were in the process of buying a new house. She was pregnant with our second child. And I had no income coming in.

My $150K per year salary dried up overnight. Back then, to me, that was a lot of money. Most of the jobs I could apply for were paying half that or less. I wasn't sure how I was going to make at least $12,500 per month, but I needed to find a way.

At that point, I did an overview of everything that was going on in my life. My lifestyle changed completely during that first year because I started questioning and scrutinizing all of the expenses. *How much is TV? How much is the energy? How much is food?* I had a spreadsheet because I love figuring all that stuff out.

I love the math of getting there, and I love saving. I've always been a saver. I used to save coins as a kid; then, I'd ask my parents to drive me to a store to buy coin rollers so that I could sit in my room and roll the coins I'd saved. I'd never count up my money until the day I rolled it. Sometimes, I'd end up with six or seven $10 rolls at once. At around nine years old, I would hide my money in the little desk in my room. At one point, I remember having a hundred and fifty bucks. It was huge for me.

My mindset was always, *You gotta start somewhere.* Every time I had to start over, I would always think, *Don't worry. Just get started. Just get it going. It'll build. And it'll build faster than you realize. Don't even think about it. Just do what you need to do.*

I almost never look at the end goal because if I do, I start to feel overwhelmed. Instead, I focus on what I need to do to get things done day by day and month by month. Then, when I look back at what I've accomplished, not only have I reached my goals but I've surpassed them.

Getting there is kind of like building a house brick by brick. Each brick needs to be placed with care or the house will fall down. But if you keep laying those bricks, eventually you will have built a massive house.

In order to save a few months of income before going all-in on my lead generation business, I started consulting. I would get a client for $10K a month, another for $5K, and another for $7,500. I was making anywhere from $15K on a low month up to $40K on a high month. I'd tell my wife Ali, "This is unbelievable!"

I was killing it. It was awesome. But I probably needed ten people to do all the stuff that I was doing. Ultimately, it was like having four or five jobs because I don't know how to do anything less than 100%. The money was great, but I wasn't getting any sleep, and the anxiety got to be too much.

The end goal for me was not to work all the time but to build a business that would bring in cash flow every day, paying dividends on the work I did months ago. I wanted to be able to work hard for 30 to 90 days then get paid on those efforts for months and years to come.

That way, I could move on to the next thing and the next thing, constantly building multiple revenue streams. I would set realistic goals, but I never put a limit on abundance.

The conservative side of me had to do the consulting to make money to set aside, but my end goal was always to build something that would free up my time. Time was more valuable to me than anything else because it's the one thing I could never get back.

I didn't know it at the time, but my mom instilled something in me that I attribute as one of the reasons for all of my success. She told me that if I believe in myself, anything is possible. She passed away when she was only 54, but her words stuck with me.

Every day, I would go over to my dad's house and work from his kitchen, rent-free and distraction-free. I put my head down and stayed focused. I kept giving myself invisible mental parachutes, so I never gave in to fear. All I knew was that I had to make at least $12,500 per month, and I naively believed I could do it. I didn't look up until I hit my goal of $150K for the year. I hit that goal in less than six months.

To my surprise—and the surprise of my wife and everyone who knew me—I eventually started making in a month what I had previously been making in a year. And that number just kept growing.

I took calculated risks, protected my mindset, found something that worked, and I scaled it. Since that time, I have stayed focused on lead generation, helping businesses scale, and I'm now in a position to be able to quit working altogether.

But life isn't just about making enough money to live comfortably. Making money gives you security, but purpose gives you the motivation to keep going. I once heard Tony Robbins, who has coached some of the wealthiest people in the world, say something about the people he worked with not having a purpose. He said that they would tell him all sorts of reasons why they wanted to work with him, but the root of all of those reasons came down to one common theme: They needed help finding their purpose in life. I still think about that today.

I could spend my days playing golf or tennis or going on vacations, but I would eventually start to feel empty. I could focus all of my attention and energy on my wife and kids, but I'd probably drive them nuts because, as an entrepreneur and former athlete, I have boundless ideas and energy.

What I've discovered is that I need a challenge, so I compete with myself. When I get really competitive, I'm intense. I'm very focused, and I go after it. For me, success has always been about mindset. I learned this while playing baseball where the game is slow.

When I was 17 and in high school, I got selected for the Junior Olympics to play baseball with 64 other kids in the country—including A-Rod (Alex Rodriquez), who was 18 at the time. Watching that kid play almost destroyed my self-confidence.

A-Rod ended up becoming one of the greatest MLB players in the history of baseball, signing two $500 million contracts. He was playing the NY Yankees in the playoffs only six months after playing with me in the Junior Olympics.

Competing against great players taught me to keep my head down and focus on my own game. It also showed me the human side of greatness, the insecurities, and the fear. Being able to experience this showed me that we put people on these pedestals when, in fact, we are all the same. I'm not saying that you could be Alex Rodriguez, but you can definitely achieve greatness if you believe in yourself and aren't afraid to fail.

I credit a lot of my success to this one principle. It is so important to "do you," and stay in your own lane. Don't worry about what others are achieving around you. Just stay focused on becoming the best version of yourself.

If you can master your mind in the midst of adversity, you can do anything you want.

Before I was able to find what worked, I spent years perfecting my media arbitrage method over the course of my career. I was able to monetize my super-connector skills to not only help businesses grow but also make customers happy.

When you figure out what your customers want, you can build a business and scale it as big as you want. But there's only one way to find out what your customers want, and that is to ask them.

Oddly enough, most business owners skip this part. But you would never dream of meeting someone through online dating and going on a date with them before first asking a few questions. If you were making dinner reservations, you would need to know what type of food they enjoy. Do they have any food allergies? What time is best? Getting those answers will help you plan an evening around your date, not around you.

Imagine going on a few dates and never asking a single question. You would never do that in a romantic relationship, right? Then why do we do this in business?

We have one-sided conversations with our audience. We place ads and design opt-in funnels, write books and publish podcasts, put out lead magnets and record webinars, *but it's all one-sided.*

A conversation only becomes a dialogue when it goes both ways. Otherwise, it's a monologue.

Most entrepreneurs are guilty of this, but they don't know how to fix it.

The solution is simple: Ask your audience what they want.

But how do you do that?

You use a survey funnel.

Survey funnels are effective for multiple reasons:

1. **Self Discovery:** We are all selfish! We love discovering new things about ourselves. We love learning why we are awesome or how we can avoid making mistakes.

2. **Self Declare:** Through a survey funnel, you can find out who your leads are, where they are, what they think, and how they behave. They will declare to you what their problem is that you need to solve.

3. **Segmentation:** Surveys and quizzes allow you to create target markets (market segmentation), giving you the ability to customize your messaging and focus on each segment's specific problem or pain point.

4. **Engagement:** You get 7 seconds to get someone's attention. Surveys and quizzes create curiosity, and that creates engagement to increase page views and get higher conversions.

5. **Cost-Effective:** Surveys will lower your cost per lead and cost per acquisition.

6. **Retargeting:** Retarget a user even if they do not opt in and give you their information. You can do this by dropping a retargeting pixel on every question and answer, which allows you to follow up with leads even if they do not opt in.

First, you create a curiosity-based headline to ATTRACT people who fit your target market profile, enabling you to split your market into smaller groups of people with similar needs and identifiable characteristics (this is market segmentation).

Then, you survey your audience, asking the right questions that allow your potential customers to self declare their skill set and tell you what their objections, fears, and insecurities are about your product or service.

By asking the right questions, you can IDENTIFY which SEGMENT the lead should be in, enabling you to have multiple TARGET markets. This allows you to create custom-tailored marketing messages, POSITIONING your offer differently for each target market segment. By doing this, you create the perception that you designed a custom plan for each person's specific needs without ever changing your core offer.

This is the Perfect Survey Method broken into five parts: Attract, Identify, Segment, Target, and Position. To help my ADHD brain remember each of the parts, I created a framework called A.I.S.T.P. Now, every time I design a survey funnel, I think of the letters A.I.S.T.P. (If you need a good mnemonic device, try making a silly sentence out of the letters. For example, "Amazon Is Selling Toilet Paper.")

When you create marketing messages that make the person feel relatable, you create a connection that shows you empathize with their specific problem. You are creating the perception that you customized the product just for them when, in fact, all you did was split your target market into different groups by the top 3–5 objections, enabling you to tailor specific messaging to break down each target market's disbeliefs without ever changing your core product.

Apple does this with the Macbook. They customize their core product for college students, families, and business owners. It's the same laptop but with different features that appeal to different market segments.

If you go to the Nike website, you'll see that they do the same thing. They segment their core offer (athletic shoes) to target men, women, and kids. Again, they're using the same core product, but they're positioning it for a niche market.

Of course, because I've been geeking out on all things lead-gen and media arbitrage since 2003, I had to create a platform for business owners to use to easily start conversations with prospective customers. What I do is kind of like online dating for businesses. I use my marketing expertise to make connections online.

The software I created is called SurveyDetective. This SaaS (software as a service) interviews the customer to find out what the customer wants. Instead of the business throwing itself at the customer, screaming, "Marry me!" SurveyDetective makes the connection and creates a dialogue—not a monologue.

It helps business owners convert ice-cold leads into customers by using specific surveys to research, segment, target, and position their products to the right person, at the right time, and the right place. I built it so that entrepreneurs who have zero tech skills can easily build survey funnels and start conversations with future customers.

This tool simplifies online marketing by providing users with pre-built survey options to easily build surveys, quizzes, assessments, and contests to build a massive list of qualified leads and turn them into customers.

When you use survey funnels, you'll be more relatable to your audience, you'll be able to understand them in a way your competitors will not. The customer experience will be better, and you'll close more business.

Obviously, you don't have to use SurveyDetective in your marketing. You can create your own survey funnels and start conversations with your customers as early as right now. But before you go making a survey funnel of your own, you'll want to avoid the biggest mistakes that most business owners make when it comes to survey funnels:

Mistake #1: Not understanding your audience. WHO you are surveying is the most important part of creating any survey.

Mistake #2: Your survey can't be completed on any device. Surveys that aren't mobile-responsive will get ignored.

Mistake #3: Asking more than one question at a time. Start with no-brainer questions to get people clicking because over 90% of people who start a survey will complete it if it's structured the right way.

Mistake #4: Asking too many questions per survey. Ask only 3–12 questions.

Mistake #5: Not providing a progress bar. Short surveys with progress bars dramatically decrease dropoff.

Mistake #6: Giving the results too early. Don't give away the results on the opt-in page! Instead, create curiosity by giving the results in an acronym (like the DISC profile, for instance), using unique terminology that is specific to your business, so the prospective customer will be curious and want to learn more.

Mistake #7: Not explaining what their result means or how they can fix it. Don't leave them hanging! That's frustrating and a recipe for getting ghosted.

Mistake #8: Not delivering the lead magnet on the outcome page. You need to give your lead what they want and fulfill on the big promise you made on the welcome page.

Mistake #9: Not having a plan. You need to know where you want to take your lead once the survey is completed. If you craft your outcome page the right way, the connection will be so strong that the person is thinking, "Wow, they get me, this is great, so what do I do next?" This is where you transition from the survey results to your survey goal (book a meeting, watch a webinar, buy a low-ticket offer, register for an event, etc.).

Mistake #10: Forgetting to FB pixel the survey funnel questions and answers for retargeting!

By avoiding these common survey mistakes, your collected data will be more accurate. Also, creating clear questions and having an understandable and complete set of answer choices leads to valuable feedback.

All in all, a well-designed survey strategy lets you kill two birds with one stone. Not only are your answers highly relevant questions but you can also use surveys to target relevant web visitors with the right CTAs. All in an unobtrusive, natural manner, which strictly relates to your leads' motivations.

Asking your customers what they want and then giving it to them is the foundation for any good business, but it doesn't stop there. What's often missing—especially for online businesses and marketers—is the follow-up.

The Fortune Is in the Follow Up

Once you've attracted your ideal customer, identified who they are, segmented them into groups based on what they want, created an offer targeted specifically to them, and positioned your solution as a customized approach to their problem, it's time to follow up.

Your goal is to ascend your customer up your value ladder, as Russell Brunson, bestselling author and co-founder of ClickFunnels, teaches. The more value you deliver, the more you can charge.

Once your customer says, "Yes!" and buys from you, they are far more likely to buy from you again (and a lot less work than acquiring a new customer), so keep the dialogue going, keep offering quality content, and you will build a loyal customer for life.

And that's how you attract, nurture, and convert cold strangers into hot customers who want to seal the deal by buying from you.

But it all starts with *asking questions* that get them talking. If you're talking *at* your customer, you'll never know what they want, and you might have a beautiful soliloquy in the form of your book or website or social media, but it means nothing without feedback. You've got to *listen* to your audience!

At Universal Performance Marketer and SurveyDetective, all of our actions, goals, projects, and programs begin and end with our customers. Everything my team and I do is focused on finding out what our customers want and making our customers happy. As Jeff Bezos said over and over again in an interview I listened to several years ago, "Obsess over your customer."

Find out what your customers want and give it to them.

Interested in learning more but not sure the best way to get started? Follow these simple steps to hit the ground running:

1. Get the Survey Software: **SurveyDetective.io**

2. Get Online Training to Fast-Track Your Success: **SurveyBuilderSecrets.io**

3. Discover More Free Content on Eric's Podcast, YouTube Channel, and Connect with Eric's Community here:

Eric.Social

CHAPTER SIX

JAMIE WOLF

Jamie Wolf

Jamie Wolf, MBA, is the CEO and President of Million Dollar Story Agency, a global agency working with entrepreneurs and leaders across industries and verticals to build their brand market authority and visibility. Specifically, she works with high achievers ready to establish themselves as the go-to expert in their space. She helps them skyrocket their credibility and authority, join the ranks of elite thought leaders, and reach a broader audience by becoming *USA Today* and *Wall Street Journal* best sellers in anthologies, done within 120 days, without even writing! She is also the founder of Wolf Tide Publishing. One hundred percent of the dozens of 6- to 9-figure entrepreneurs who have chosen to work with Million Dollar Story Agency have hit #1 Best seller; their books have then stayed in the Top 25–100 for 12+ months. A multiple bestselling author herself, she also hosts the *MILLION DOLLAR PIVOT* podcast.

ELEVATE YOUR MARKET BRAND AUTHORITY EXPONENTIALLY

The pit in my stomach felt like a bowling ball. Walking into the event space, I felt like a sucker for dropping more money than I had spent on my previous car. What if I had just fallen for a sales pitch made by an experienced closer? What if this was a total waste of time, money, and energy?

My inner critic had plenty of time to beat me down as I flew from Savannah to Philadelphia and drove to the hotel. I had no idea what to expect. I just knew that a door had opened for me, and I felt an invisible nudge to go through it.

The keynote speaker for the mastermind event I was about to attend was Jack Canfield, co-creator of the *Chicken Soup for the Soul* series. I was excited to finally be in the same room and hopefully get to meet him—especially because my cousin, Tim Clauss, had contributed to the book *Chicken Soup for the Soul at Work* and had his photo featured on the back cover. But even my familial tie to Canfield didn't assuage my fears of being out of my league.

Outwardly, I kept up appearances. Nobody would question my work ethic. Inwardly, though, my confidence was shaky at best. I wasn't yet living my life with purpose. But there I was—betting on myself—because something in me just wouldn't give up.

At that point, life had presented more than its fair share of challenges. My friends and I would often say, "What doesn't kill you makes you stronger" and follow it up with, "Alright! Enough already!"

I went to this event because I wanted to learn how to write and market a book that would turn those stories of test after test into a solution-oriented message for others. Deep down, I secretly hoped the process would also bring me some redemption.

The voice in my head—you know, the constant critic—kept asking: *Who are you to write a book? Who would ever gain value from your words? You can barely make a difference in your own life. Who do you think you are to try to make a difference in someone else's? You're destined to FAIL.*

To say I was shocked when I walked into that room would be an understatement. What I saw took my breath away. The room was packed with at least 500 people who had all invested in themselves and their futures the way I had. I wasn't alone!

I made some long-lasting friendships and, in fact, I am still friends today with some of the people I met in that room years ago. But what I learned at that event has shaped the course of my life ever since.

What I learned is this: Writing a memoir because you "want to write a book one day" is very different from writing a strategic book with purpose—especially if you're an entrepreneur.

After that event, I walked through another open door. And then another. And then another.

And that's how I ended up at my first Funnel Hacking Live. It's where I met my business partner, Angela, and my network. It's when I finally found the secret to tying all the pieces of my life experiences together to produce results for myself and others.

This path has led me to a life not only of profit but also of purpose—and a Million Dollar Identity.

Today, I am so fortunate to hear stories from courageous entrepreneurs who appear to be overnight successes but who have all fought a good fight to achieve their status. I have the privilege of being the conduit to get those stories out into the world to make a difference and serve others.

I laugh and cry often as I meet exceptional entrepreneurs driven to start a movement of transformation. It compels me to do better, learn more, and reach higher.

But I didn't start out this way...

At 2:00 a.m. one Thanksgiving morning, I rushed my daughter unconscious—all 65 pounds of her—to the ER, where she was diagnosed with Type 1 diabetes.

I will never forget that early morning nightmare. She had been wearing a choker made from little beads with letters spelling her name. After trying to get an IV line into her arms, her hands, her feet, they gave up and decided to use a jugular catheter.

I was living out a TV show drama where the ER team rushes about and pushes family members aside. I felt that I was in the way, relegated to watching helplessly as they worked from all angles on her little limp body, when, without hesitation, they cut her choker from her neck. Each letter of her name fell in slow motion to the floor, bouncing and scattering in all directions.

PAMELA

That slow-motion fragmentation was to become a metaphor for my life, the visible destruction of everything I had held dear or thought I could control up to that point.

Thankfully, they were able to stabilize her and transport her to another hospital, where she spent three days in the ICU. She came home to a new life for herself, her older brother, and me—a life revolving around Type 1 diabetes.

As I searched for ways to help my daughter, I understood there were possible solutions to improving the lives of people with chronic diseases. It wasn't long before I co-founded a company with my husband at the time to help people manage their diabetes. Within 18 months, we got a product cleared by the U.S. Food and Drug Administration, and we continued to raise millions of dollars from angel capital investors.

One day, I got a call from our COO telling me to meet at a coffee shop in an hour. When I arrived, I was surprised to see him joined by my husband. Both were looking grim. They pulled out a letter of resignation and pushed it across the table, forcing me to sign it or be fired immediately.

It got worse.

Within 24 hours, I learned that our joint bank accounts had been closed—and emptied. Shortly after that, my husband announced he was divorcing me. I was dumbfounded. Without a safety net, I had plummeted from a multi-six-figure income to unemployed.

Life was bleak.

After two months of struggling to make ends meet as well as buy insulin and diabetes supplies for my daughter, my husband took my younger son—who was just six years old at the time—from me. Nathaniel was crying and reaching out for me. That's when I hit rock bottom. Completely and utterly broken, I sat there, sobbing, until there was nothing left.

Wave after wave of grief washed over me, but I was faced with two choices: Give up or start over again.

I decided to start over.

The road to starting over began over a decade ago. Today, I am grateful for the bond I have with my three children. My daughter is healthy and managing her Type 1 diabetes with grace and courage. We're able to look back at those years with gratitude that we survived. Today, we choose to thrive.

We all face hurdles, disappointments, and failures. If we're open, those challenges can teach us grace and gratitude. Without the lows, we can't appreciate the highs. Without the ability to overcome obstacles, we can't grow. Without experiencing setbacks, we can't be proud of our resilience and capabilities. And if we don't stumble, we can't learn to reach out to others for help.

Personal tragedies and professional betrayals can—if we let them—serve to remind us how precious every moment and every good relationship can be. We always have a choice in how we hold what happens to us or for us.

What is exquisite about the journey to a Million Dollar Identity is I get to feel compassion for the person I used to be and grateful for the lessons that helped me grow into who I have become. Plus, the journey isn't finished! These days I choose to work with other mission-driven entrepreneurs to help them share with a focus on ROI—through stories and business—their Million Dollar Identities.

What my mentor, Russell Brunson, has said over and over again is to focus on *one* thing until you generate $1 million with one funnel. To that end, my agency shows experts how to leverage one of the most powerful business tools to increase revenue and audience reach in record time: #1 bestselling books.

A book is a powerful business tool that, when done strategically, fulfills the five factors that are essential for EVERY profitable business. We call this the Profit Pentagon™, and it includes:

1. Lead Generation & Prospecting

2. Lead Nurture & Relationship Building

3. Lead Conversion & Sales

4. Client Delivery & Fulfillment

5. Client Retention & Ascension

Using a proven, repeatable system, we help experts not only write and publish bestselling books in 90 days, but we also help them architect their business assets, set up their team, establish inexpensive traffic systems, and craft a clear and compelling message. (And for those too busy to write, we have a 100% Done For You process, too.)

A bestselling book creates instant celebrity status, credibility, and brand market authority for the author. Previously invisible entrepreneurs have become seemingly overnight successes after announcing and promoting their #1 best seller.

Leveraging clear and well-crafted front-end offers, core offers, and high-ticket offers, a bestselling book can boost profits in record time. Once the Million Dollar Story Agency authors have all of their systems in place, we show them how to turn on the faucet to generate a never-ending supply of new leads that turn into raving fans and, ultimately, loyal customers.

Million Dollar Story Agency ensures that the systems are in place for a successful launch that is set up for scale. We strongly encourage all our authors to provide stellar customer service to everyone who buys their book because satisfied customers become loyal and hungry fans who want the next thing and the next, ascending the value ladder, and buying increasingly higher ticket offers. They leave 5-star reviews, record glowing video testimonials, and gladly refer you to others because success sells.

With a never-ending pipeline of new clients, entrepreneurs get to do what they love best. Whether that's making the offers, coaching the clients, running the masterminds, building the funnels, installing the software, setting up the ad campaigns, shipping the products, giving the speeches, hosting the events, enjoying the time freedom ... The possibilities are endless.

When it comes to writing a book, though, the first thing you need to do is to define what success looks like to you. Understand and be able to talk about why you want to write a book. Try to visualize the end from the beginning.

People who work with me find that writing either a chapter in an anthology or their own solo-authored book increases their clarity around their offer. It positions them as the go-to person in their niche. And it provides a way for prospects to get to know, like, and trust them through their stories.

The key is to think of a book as a vehicle that picks up cold traffic and delivers it to you as warm traffic. After your prospects read your stories, they have transformed into a warm audience, ready to buy from you because they can relate to you. They see themselves in your journey, and they believe you can and will help them.

Now, if your audience is made up of busy entrepreneurs, then you will need to provide an audiobook version as well as an e-book and a print book. Understand that different people consume information in different ways, so it's important to cater to your specific audience.

Million Dollar Story Agency works with experts—entrepreneurs, consultants, speakers, coaches, CEOs, and business owners—who have an offer and who recognize that a book is an excellent evergreen lead generation tool.

At the end of your book, you'll want to offer a chance to work with you directly. Create a compelling call to action that leads to an irresistible offer. That way, the book leads them into your value ladder.

When a reader or prospect adds their name to your email list, you can continue to nurture them and provide value. That way, you stand out as someone who actually provides solutions to their pain.

If you have a high-ticket course or group mastermind, organize your content in such a way that it mirrors what you're already doing. If you don't have a course, then you can conserve your time and energy by crafting your book and course simultaneously. It's possible to build out your entire business infrastructure of front-end and back-end offers at once, within 90 days, while creating the systems and processes to master organic traffic and team building.

Authors who use books as their front-end offer say that they're able to head off objections about their core and high-ticket offers prior to any closing calls, which reduces customer acquisition cost and time.

They also find that they position themselves as the #1 authority in their market. (There's a reason the word "author" is in the word "authority.")

A well-planned book strategy can lead to several outcomes, including:

- An evergreen lead gen/prospecting tool

- A lead nurture system so prospects get to know, like, and trust you

- A lead conversion system so cold leads are warmed up as they read your book

- An increase in conversion rates

- A decrease in conversion costs

- A client delivery/fulfillment system

- A sales funnel that includes at least three offers—for example, a free lead magnet (a free + shipping book), digital assets (e-book), an order bump (audiobook), an OTO (one-time offer for a challenge), a DIY course, a group coaching program, a high-ticket mastermind …

- Client retention and ascension—happy customers who become raving lifelong fans

- A completed e-book

- A completed print book

- A completed audiobook

- A published book

- A launched book

- Amazon or *USA Today/WSJ* best seller status as a published author

- A process to monetize based on your book

- Increased brand awareness

- Elevated authority

- Personal fulfillment because YOU DID IT!

Becoming a published bestselling author also helps you develop your influence and your relationships with colleagues, prospects, and clients. Your opportunities expand significantly through one or more of the following:

- Increased press exposure—magazines, radio, TV, and more

- Invitations to podcasts

- Invitations to summits

- Invitations to speaking events

- Opportunities for affiliate work, joint ventures, and possible partnerships

Scaling from 6-figure years to 6-figure months and from 6-figure months to 8-figure years is much easier with a book, a system, and a sales funnel. We've seen published, bestselling authors take quantum leaps in their business.

Achieving an Amazon Best Seller is an excellent launch point. But business owners who choose to become *USA Today* and *WSJ* best-selling authors identify as high achievers who want to reach a broader audience. By establishing themselves as the go-to expert in their space, they join the ranks of elite thought leaders.

They know that climbing to the top of those charts will skyrocket their credibility and market brand authority. Topping the charts makes it even easier for you to charge a premium for your offers and speaking engagements, and it opens the door for you to get invited to higher-level podcasts, summits, events, and networks. It can also pave the way to TEDx speaking opportunities or getting Verified (blue checkmark) on IG and FB.

Once they have grown their influence, audience, and revenue, that's when author-entrepreneurs are positioned to create a movement, make a significant impact, and build a legacy for their family.

Over a lifetime of work, I've functioned as a student, hourly employee, corporate manager, consultant, tech start-up co-founder, syndicated columnist, author, publisher, marketing agency owner, real estate investor, and owner of a boxing gym.

What emerged from all those experiences is a passion for helping success-driven and mission-driven entrepreneurs make a much greater impact by telling their stories in a way that significantly grows their influence, audience, and revenue.

I help busy industry leaders become #1 on lists that matter with minimal disruption from their busy schedules, and I get them published fast to elevate their market authority, brand, visibility, credibility, and influence. I also help experts use the process of creating those books to build their entire business infrastructure to scale their business.

If that sounds like you, and you would like for us to help you write, publish, and market a strategic book that grows your business and increases your impact—potentially even creating a high-ticket offer that puts you on the path to your own Million Dollar Identity fast— then book a call with our team and let's connect:

MillionDollarStory.co

CHAPTER SEVEN

KEENAN WILLIAMS

Keenan Williams

Keenan Williams, aka @papichulo_dreaded with 1.3M followers on IG, is the founder of Ko Elixir, a skincare company that specializes in creams for cellulite and stretch marks. At the helm of a multimillion dollar company that is only three years old, Keenan has used the power of affiliate marketing and Instagram advertising to bring visibility to his company and drive revenue. He also runs a coaching program called NextBracket4U.com, where he shares how to get into the next tax bracket by starting and maintaining a successful e-commerce business.

BECOME A MASTER
OF INFINITE SCALE

It was one of the scariest days of my life. I was working a shift at Skechers when I got a text from my sister: MOM JUST HAD A STROKE GET TO THE HOSPITAL ASAP. I was in complete shock, but I knew that I had to go be with my mom. I knew that a stroke was really serious. What if she died?

Crying, I went up to my boss and told him what had happened and that I needed to leave. He looked at me and said, "Do you know what day it is? It's Saturday. The busiest day of the week. Go back out there and sell some shoes." So many thoughts raced through my head. *How could this guy be such a jerk? I'm a hard worker. I've always been a hard worker. And all I've ever wanted from anybody was respect.*

But I didn't feel like I received it that day.

I was at a crossroads. I could sit back and let my boss control my life, or I could take control and move my life in a different direction. I knew what I had to do. So I left. Driving to the hospital, I was filled with a sense of clarity. I left so that I could be with my mom, first and foremost. But I also realized just how much power a person can have over your livelihood. Just like that, I didn't have a job. Because I wanted to be with my mom when she needed me the most.

I have to admit that I did think for a split second about staying at work. I was a single father at the time. I dropped out of high school. I was only making $8/hour, but at least I was making something. My mom is still alive as I write this, but if she had died and I had stayed at work—I wouldn't have been able to forgive myself.

That was the day that forever changed my life. I made a vow that I would no longer let someone else control my, or my family's, future. I knew that I had to create my own source of income so that I would no longer have to put up with being disrespected by someone in a position of authority over me. And that's how my curiosity for entrepreneurship got started.

I started with just $300—my last Skechers paycheck—and I'm now an eight-figure earner. I know what it's like to go from being broke, living paycheck to paycheck, to literally making money while I sleep. It did take time to get where I am today. Each milestone pushed me to keep going. That first $300 pushed me to the next $300. I used to think that a $300 paycheck was amazing money. I would wake up every day and thank God for what I had.

With my own business, I started seeing $5,000 and $10,000 days. That much money in *one day*. I recently woke up to $200,000 in one day. A six-figure day! Through being my own boss, I learned that what I previously thought was impossible is actually very possible.

Not only have I achieved eight figures in earnings in my skincare company the past three years, but I have also created 26 millionaires through my coaching program in the last year and a half. My students have been successful across multiple industries. The one thing that they all have in common is that they're running e-commerce businesses, selling digital or physical goods online.

I consider myself an e-commerce guru. People come to me because I have been successful, and I show them step-by-step how to find the same success. But they also want to work with me because I am re-latable. My introduction to entrepreneurship was affiliate marketing, selling someone else's product for them. I lost money doing that. I've been broke three times. I've had money and then lost it *three different times*. I've made mistakes. I've learned countless lessons. And I've seen huge outcomes.

A lot of my students also don't have much money to get their businesses going. Just like me when I was starting. I think that's a really important part of my success; people want to work with someone who they can relate to, someone who has been where they've been.

I've experienced a lot in the four or five years that I've been on this journey. The neighborhood that we were living in before I started my business was rough. There were people getting shot every day, and we'd have to lie to our kids and tell them it's fireworks, it's the 4th of July, even though it's the middle of August.

I moved away from Montgomery, Alabama, for a better life. Still, all I could afford was low-income housing. It wasn't until I met my wife that everything started to click. Before I met her, I didn't feel like I had an identity of my own at all. I was just another person on the conveyor belt. A cog in the machine. Never getting off, never checking to see where I was going. My wife gave me a reason to want to be better.

I always wanted a family when I was younger, to be a father. I wanted to be a provider. I wanted to be somebody's everything. I saw how my mom looked at my dad. She had three teenagers, and my dad had so much love for my mom's children. I learned a lot from my parents. They worked together—my mom was an apartment manager, and my dad worked in maintenance. I learned management from my mom and hard work from my dad.

I helped them out. I learned how to work, how to sell. I didn't realize that I had been preparing to be an entrepreneur my whole life. I tell people all the time; we've been selling our entire lives. We just don't always realize what form of selling we're doing.

I learned how to be a professional closer early on. But most people do that work for others, and it's misplaced. Putting in the hours at your 9-5, structured lunch breaks, knowing the work you need to do every day and how to prioritize it. It's amazing when you can make a shift to doing those things for your own business.

E-commerce literally changed my life. I never knew how much money was out there, especially for someone like me who doesn't have a high school degree. I always thought you had to go to Harvard to make millions of dollars. When I was making retail money, 6- or 7-figures in a day felt impossible. But e-commerce is a whole different ball game. The internet, unlike the rest of the world, has no face, no bias. Anybody can come into this space and create a successful business.

Without a physical storefront, you don't have to depend on foot traffic alone. Foot traffic is a thing of the past, really. With the COVID pandemic, a lot of people are reluctant to go into physical stores. So businesses that are only brick and mortar are struggling, while online businesses are thriving. And that trend will continue.

With e-commerce, orders come in constantly from people all over the world. You can get paid 24/7. While I'm writing this chapter, I'm getting paid. While I'm sleeping, I'm getting paid. While I'm spending time with my family, I'm getting paid. It's amazing.

Over a trillion dollars is going to be made this year alone in e-commerce businesses. And these are small businesses, like mine, competing with the big dogs, the bigger stores and markets. E-commerce gives the little guy power.

Giant industry leaders come to me and ask to pay me to teach their employees. I always say no. This is power that hasn't been given out fairly over the course of decades. There have been times when people haven't gotten work if they were a woman or a person of color. People can be quick to judge you based on your background as well. Like, "Did you go to college? No? Well, I'm not gonna give you this loan to open a business."

The power of social media is evident. In my company, we market everything on social media. Social media is the oil in the engine. All you need to do is learn *how* to market, which I teach in my program as well. I teach how to partner with influencers, so you can get your brand out into the world before even building an audience. You don't have to build an audience yourself. I didn't build an audience myself. I leveraged influencers who have put in years dedicated to their audience to push my brand.

And you can go beyond online. I have many students who have their products in stores because the stores see their social media presence and know that carrying their products will bring new customers into their store. So if you're willing to do wholesale deals, you can expand from B2C (business to customer) to B2B (business to business). E-commerce can open you up to a whole new world of income. Starting with social media marketing is sure to set you up for success.

Being on social media will help you understand the terrain of your industry and what's missing. It will help you understand what your customer wants. I tell all my students: Give your customers quality, and they will make you rich.

You are selling a problem, not a product. You're asking them questions about their problem. Get them to the point where they're saying, "Yes, yes, yes, yes, yes. What do you have for my problem?"

Once you've identified the problem, overexplained the problem, and made people *very* aware of the problem, then you sell the problem with your product. And make the problem so evident that people will spend whatever it takes to fix it. That is how my company sees results so quickly.

It's about convenience. You can make millions in e-commerce off of convenience. When someone opens their social media, you want to be the first thing that they see, whether it's through ads or influencers.

And you need to position your content as if you are talking to one person. Even if you have 10,000 followers, you're not communicating with everybody. You're communicating with one person. Building a close relationship with the individual is what drives sales.

I want to tell you about the first millionaire in my coaching program, Mike Kimbrough. This happened within the first year of launching my program. It only cost $20/month when he joined. He was very quiet, and he only had $150, but he was committed to doing the work. He wrote down word for word what I said in my videos. He showed up to every single live call. He mirrored everything that I did. He told me at one point, "I had to live and breathe what you were saying." And he started seeing results. Three months into the program, he made $100,000. Around the 11-month period, he hit $1 million.

Mike threw a party in celebration, just as I had done when my company first hit $1 million. We shared a beautiful moment at his party—words of affirmation, positivity, and congratulations. We hugged, and we cried. He told me that he almost felt like a son to me because I ushered him to places he never dreamed he could go.

Mike's million-dollar moment let everyone else in the program know that it's possible. But his success also showed me what I was capable of. Up until then, I didn't know what would happen. I hoped it would work for people. That showing them how to build their own e-commerce business would bring them success. The hopes of every coach. But nobody really knows if their program will help anyone until they have a successful student.

When that happened, the confidence surged through me. I wanted to keep doing this for other people. Mike gave me credibility. And the rest of the world listened. Close to 10,000 people joined my program after they saw Mike's success. They saw that it was possible.

E-commerce will surpass $1 trillion this year, which is huge money during a pandemic. The surge has been crazy—to the point where I went from doing $300,000/month in revenue to over a million-plus in revenue each month. And it's not going to slow down. COVID proved that people feel safer shopping at home. So all you have to do as an e-commerce business is get your products in front of people's faces—on their social media feed. The formula that I teach my students is that you need a product that runs out every 30 days and that's infinitely scalable.

You can learn how to do this in my NextBracket4U program. For $50/month, my students have unlimited access to classes that will help them start and grow a business. In my $5,000/year program, I share how to break into the top four cash cow businesses that are blowing up in e-commerce. I'm talking billion-dollar industries. I've made 6- to 7-figures in each of these four industries, and I teach people how to get started and exactly what to sell.

I take the guesswork out of it because some people get stuck on what to sell. They have the drive, and they want to succeed, but they just can't think of a product. This high-end program will always be one of the most valuable programs that I offer. The most important thing is putting in the work—taking the information that I am providing and implementing it. I have had students who made their money back within two to three weeks of joining the program. There is such demand for these products. I want to help people have the same success that I have had. There is enough e-commerce profit to go around for those who know which industries to tap into and who put in the hard work. And that's what I offer in my programs.

What makes my courses special is that I don't just talk about money. I talk about how to structure your life. I share personal stories about my wife and me. There's a video on self-betterment. It's almost a life coaching aspect that I offer. At the beginning of a business launch, it's easy to get into a funk and not know what to do next.

Do you trust your business, or do you not? At first, I didn't trust my business. But you have to. It wasn't until I trusted myself to put my all into the business that I started making money. You have to dive in, get to work, and realize that there is greatness inside of you.

I believe we all have a poor part and a rich part of our brains. The rich part is what makes you take an idea and start building a brand and a business. The rich part comes to fruition when you listen and steer down that path. The poor part of your brain is listening to everybody else who is skeptical or saying you can't do it or asking how do you have the money or the time or whatever it is. The poor part of your brain listens to the doubters and the haters.

It's not even that people don't wish better for you. They're fine with you winning, but they want to win more or first. People will project their fears and insecurities onto you. Don't let them. Students come into the live calls with excitement and curiosity and fear, and I tell them, "You got this." I remind them how long they've wanted to start their own business or break free from a job they hate that overworks them, or that doesn't care about their well-being. I remind them that this will feed their family, that this will give them more time and freedom.

I don't know what other avenue could grant this much freedom. I am doing the work that I want to do, *and* I bought my time back. That's what I believe that e-commerce can grant everybody. It will allow you to buy your time back. If you're willing to put in the work upfront, just like you have with other jobs, you'll get huge benefits, buying back your time with the money that you make. And now you can be the person that you really want to be.

If you want someone to take the guesswork out of e-commerce and give you the exact steps it takes to build a multimillion dollar e-commerce business, find me at the link below. I map out everything you need to know about what to buy, how to set it up, and how to get products that are infinitely scalable. It's time.

NextBracket4U.com

CHAPTER EIGHT

DR. HERMANIE PIERRE

Dr. Hermanie Pierre

An undercover billionaire spirit from one of the poorest countries in the world, Dr. Hermanie Pierre became a mother to her mother at age 8. Before the age of 30, she became a millionaire. Crowned Miss Haiti International, Hermanie has turned her beauty knowledge into a multi-pageant franchise ownership business. Today, she is a civil engineer, real estate investor, and business coach. She took her setbacks and turned them into income streams. Now she teaches others to do the same.

THE MONEY TREE MYTH

When I was only eight years old, my mom developed a sickness that no one could explain, so I had to become a mother to my mother. She would get up on a beautiful day, filled with spirit, making jokes, and having a great time. Then out of nowhere, she would stand still, staring into space, and we would literally have 30 to 45 seconds to jump up and grab her before she would lose consciousness and fall. She became very delusional and was having three to four seizures a day.

Her sickness started when I was three years old, but God gave me five years to "be a kid" before I had to take on the responsibility at age eight of caring for her and my baby sister, Regine. I had no idea how to figure out her illness or how to take care of her. I wasn't prepared for it, but I was obedient, and I listened to God. I trusted that He would give me the tools I needed.

Before my mother became sick, she was a teacher. She was a mother to her students, making sure they got good grades and caring deeply about them. Now, my mother couldn't work, so I had to figure out how to feed our family and pay the bills.

Each of my mom's sisters had their own business, so I decided to spend time with each of them to learn all I could about the business world.

My Aunty Magareth was a talented designer. All you had to do was show her a picture of an outfit, and she could make it for you. She didn't even need your measurements. I had no idea how she did that.

My Aunty Rose had a huge grocery boutique, and my Aunty Tise was a reseller—she would buy shoes and trending outfits and resell them for a profit. She was also the spiritual leader. She and Rose would close their shops at noon to go and pray.

My Aunty Solange focused on selling wholesale to vendors who would then sell the items for retail. Name it, and she had it. She was Amazon for us.

My Aunty Adeline was the junk food master. She made food in the mornings and sold it in the afternoon. She was like our version of McDonald's.

My Aunty Liliane was another talented designer/artist. She made hand-made crochet, tablecloths, bedsheets, and anything dealing with home décor.

And my grandma BéBé was the master of business principles. She walked 20 miles to her restaurant, where she specialized in cornmeal smoothies that we called "Akasan."

So I guess it wasn't a surprise that I decided to start my own business. The challenge was how fast I could learn it since we had bills to pay. I knew I wouldn't fail because all my aunties would help me if I needed them to.

I started my first business by selling sugarcane. I chose sugarcane not only because of the health benefits but also because growing up around elders, you quickly learn about herbs and their benefits. I heard them say that sugarcane is good for your immune system and gives you energy, and everywhere you go, someone is eating sugarcane. It was a hot-selling item, especially in the town my grandma lived in, but not as much in my town.

I needed someone to take me to market, so my Aunty Rose took me. On the way there, she advised me: Never accept the seller price but negotiate everything until they say no like ten times, and don't let them take advantage of you. She said that they were not going to take me seriously and that they would ridicule me. Remember, I was eight years old! She said to stay firm in my price and be willing to walk away if they don't want to work with me.

We got to the market, and Aunty Rose made me go by myself. I walked up to a man, told him I was starting my business, and asked the price for a dozen pieces of his best, longest sugarcane. I needed them to be as long as possible so I could cut them into small portions and have more to sell. I told him that I would be a loyal customer and buy only from him. I negotiated my price down so low that the man smiled and said, "You will be a great businesswoman."

He screamed at his friends/competitors that I was his customer for life. All the men started laughing, and I whispered to him, "Please don't be sick. Can you promise me you will be here every day?"

He replied, "My daughter, I will be here every day in God's name." He cut the sugarcane for me, tied them, and helped me put them on my head.

I walked over to my aunt, and she said, "How did you do? How much did you pay for the sugarcane?"

I told her and she said that was three times less than what she paid. I asked her what else she gave him besides negotiating the price? She said that was it. I told her that I had given him more; I made him a promise. Isn't that worth more than money? I told him he would be my only vendor. Even if he gets sick, I won't buy from his friends.

She was impressed but asked if I would take this business seriously because when you make a promise, you must keep it. These men in these small towns can kill you if you lie to them. Lying is like stealing. I told her I had every intention of keeping my promise. I will work hard to sell my sugarcane and get up early to pick out the juiciest pieces to sell for a profit.

My cousin MéMé had a very successful business selling charcoal that he made. I begged him to show me how, and I started selling with him on the weekends. I became his negotiator, and I got good at it because I learned the law of buying low and selling high. Although the food vendors needed charcoal to run their businesses, they would complain about the price to try to get it cheaper. I would explain the value of our charcoal—how it was made from the best trees and how large the pieces of charcoal were compared to others.

Even though I was young, I became known as a tough negotiator. I told them all the value points and said if they didn't want to buy, we were OK not selling to them. They always ended up buying two or three sacks. Then I started making my own batch and selling it at a higher profit than my cousin.

My grandmother was a farmer. She grew all her vegetables, rice, and almost everything you can think of. I used to farm with her and go to the public market and sell her products to other vendors. I got really good at selling. I did that until I started my own little grocery store.

My grandma was my rock. Without her, I could not take care of my mom. She taught me everything from cooking to cleaning and how to be the businesswoman with integrity that I am today. She treated me like her grandchild but raised me like a woman. She said I had to learn fast so I could do a good job with my mom.

While I was running all these businesses and taking care of my mom and my little sister, I still had to go to school. The goal was always to get straight A's. Nothing else would do.

Education in Haiti is a currency. It means respect, and respect will lead you to a better life. I knew how lucky I was to be able to attend school.

Not everyone could afford to go. So, I had no reason to complain. My situation wasn't an excuse. So many people did not have the opportunity that I had, but I had to figure life out fast. I was a kid living with adult responsibilities. I prayed every day that God would help me get to America.

My father went to America when I was very young. He would come home in the summer for two weeks when he had a vacation from his job in the US. He was working as a management supervisor and saved all his money so he could one day bring us all to the US. America was the dream for us. I constantly prayed to God that he would help us get there.

Finally, God answered our prayers, and dad was able to bring us to America, the land of opportunity.

There was a story in Haiti that America has a money tree. All you must do is go under it and money will flow all over you. I always wanted to come to America to go visit that tree and bring plenty of money back home to Haiti to share with other families. But when I moved to the US, I realized the story wasn't true.

When I came to America, I did not speak the language. I spoke three languages, but English was not one of them, so I had to learn it. I attended school and took an ESL (English as a Second Language) class.

While in school, I was bullied, and other students took advantage of me. Deep down in my heart, I knew I was the smartest kid, but I didn't have the means yet to converse in this new country. I had to give myself grace and remind myself that I hadn't learned much about the American culture in Haiti, so I was not prepared for this experience.

My goal was to get good grades because nobody could take that education away from me. Education was all the currency that I had. I also started working at Domino's Pizza so I could help my father with expenses. I needed to take care of my grandmother back home in Haiti as well.

I was learning to trade my time for money. I was happy that I could help my parents. I was invited to participate in a genius program, which was an engineering program where you must take college courses and make straight A's so you could possibly end up with a scholarship. Only a few were selected. I still did not speak English, but I was not about to let any excuses keep me from trying for this scholarship because earning a scholarship means respect, and respect means currency. My education was on the line.

I met my best friend, Briana, who was also in the program. She was an angel sent from above as she was the only one in the program who understood every single word I said. She became my interpreter. She was also the first person to give me the confidence to know that if people wanted to understand me, they would. Briana is still my best friend to this day. Whenever she is around me, I feel a sense of peace.

Well, God blessed me. At the end of the program, not only did I end up with a full four-year scholarship, but I also was able to learn how to leverage my intellectual property to get another 17 scholarships by submitting essays.

I leveraged my scholarships, got a job, and bought my first quarter-of-a-million-dollar house at age 20 without speaking proper English. That was a big deal to me. I still have this home that I keep as a rental. I leveraged money to buy it, and now I am earning money from it.

At that moment, I started to understand how the American system works, exchanging time for money or leveraging your intellectual property. I was all about leveraging to take care of my family.

Four and a half years later, I graduated and became a civil and environmental engineer with a minor in business. I was the first Haitian

American with that degree. It had been a dream in our family for generations, back from my great-great-grandfather. It had always been the men in the family with the dream, so when I was born, I felt like my father lost hope.

It wasn't until after my graduation that my father told me the story. We both laughed and cried at the same time, and I told him all it takes is a woman to break the cycle. And I told him that the same generation would create a multi-millionaire in the family.

Engineering is a male-dominant field. To be a female engineer was not easy, but all I knew was that being an engineer was something that I had always wanted to be. I learned along the way to create my destiny no matter how bad things get. I had a blueprint, and I was going to follow it. I learned a lot in college and that helped me gain experience on how to leverage everything that comes my way.

My father told me that I had three things that would hold me back. He said, "You are black, English is not your language, and you are a woman." But I have turned them into the greatest assets in my life.

The engineering job was the first step, but I knew I was just getting started. I wanted to open more doors for the next generation.

Being in such a male-dominated industry, I was told very often that I was beautiful. I know God gives us gifts for a reason, and I wanted to use this one for good. I met a woman named Wilda who was a beautiful Haitian. She told me that she had been competing in pageants for years and that I should give it a try. She said that there are many different types of pageants, so I could find one that fit me.

I decided to jump into one of the top five biggest ones. You know they say, "Go big or go home." I won Miss Spirit and Best Body.

I entered other pageants and became Miss Haiti. This changed my life, and I wanted to help more women celebrate themselves in this aspect.

So I contacted the owners of the pageant. I met with them and asked them how I could start in this business. They gave me my first shot, and I ran with it. I started with three franchises and ended up with twenty. I learned so much about how to run a business. The pageants became my babies, and I loved what I was doing. This is where I learned to master leveraging in business.

Leverage and experience are not things you can learn overnight. It takes time. In my program, I help entrepreneurs transform their setbacks into streams of income. Anyone can learn that but not everyone does it. Most complain and don't act.

As you can see, I've been fighting battles from a very young age, but not one time did I let that make me want to quit. I have always turned my situations into leverage. If you listen to me (yes, I still have an accent) and do everything I tell you to do, you can win, too. You can have a better life. At the least, you'll find some value and you can create another stream of income with what I'm sharing with you.

I want to see women earn their spot in the industry. Therefore, I created my five-day Make More Money challenge to help entrepreneurs understand their business and to teach them how to start their business the proper way. In this program, we cover business structure, business contracts, OPM (other people's money), how to leverage business credit, and how to have it all. My business mentees started referring to me as their business coach. For me, I am impacting as many souls as I can. If I can do it, anyone can.

Remember where you are now is not where you are going to end up. The only one stopping you from your dream is you. See, sometimes we hear a lot, we read a lot, but we don't take action. Everything is about taking action. So, the education is on me; the execution is on you. Your result is always going to be attached to you. One thing you need to understand is this: Everything is about principle.

As we come to an end, I will leave you with three questions. If you want your business to be successful, you must ask yourself these three questions:

1. Who are you fighting this for?

2. Who are you fighting this with?

3. What is the solution that you are bringing to the table?

Once you get those answers, you'll be able to impact the world. Trust me, we all want the gift that God has given to you. We want to hear it. We want to see it. We want to be part of it. But we can't be part of it if you don't share it with us. And finally, take time to reflect on who you are, what you are, and whose you are.

I challenge you to bring the fire inside of you out today. Start with one thing that can get you closer to your dream. Fight for your why. Remember in the beginning when I told you the story about the money tree? I did find it, just not in the form I thought it would be. It does exist, and they did not lie. I love you guys!

MMMInYourBizChallenge.com

CHAPTER NINE

KELLY JEFFERSON

Kelly Jefferson

Kelly Jefferson, aka "Coach Kelly J," is an Executive and Peak Performance Leadership Coach and the founder and CEO of Jefferson Academy of Mentorship & Life Coaching Certification, a program that trains, mentors, and certifies life coaches. She is certified in neuro-linguistic programming and holds a master's certification in Life and Business Coaching.

Coach Kelly was mentored by some of the most esteemed leaders in the coaching business, including Myron Golden, Nehemiah Davis, and Frank Kern. For the past eight years, she has garnered extensive experience in coaching top-level coaches in a wide range of industries.

She has become known as "The Coaches Coach," teaching others how to transition from a one-to-one business model to teaching their clients in groups to increase influence, impact, and income while creating time freedom.

STEP INTO YOUR DIVINE ASSIGNMENT AND CREATE THE LIFE YOU WANT

All my years of college, the six-figure salary "dream job" with the Department of Justice, and the 401K meant nothing when I was told that my request to work remotely was not approved by management.

I sat there thinking, **"Is this MY life?"** I did everything the "success blueprint" said to do: Go to college, get a good job, get married, have 2.5 kids, and buy a house with a white picket fence.

That day in my outdated cubicle with boring gray fabric walls, I felt I'd been lied to about what being successful really means. Like, how could I consider myself "successful" if I had to ask permission from another adult to take a day off or take a vacation only when it fits into their schedule? Even worse, having to get approval from my boss to take my kids to the doctor or submit a doctor's note if I would be out more than three days.

I began to wonder … WHO made these rules and WHY is this the accepted formula for success?

Although I hated it when my husband, AJ, who has been a full-time entrepreneur since the '90s, used to tease and call me a "government robot," I realized at that moment that's exactly what I was. My life and all the things that truly mattered were determined, decided, and dictated by someone other than ME.

In my mind, I just *knew* I couldn't leave. This is what I went to college to do. None of my friends even landed a job that aligned with their degree. I did … and everyone would think I was crazy if I did anything other than work there for 40 years, have a cheesy retirement party, get the cheap gold watch they give you, retire, and die a few years later because my identity revolved around my job title or position in the organization.

Here's the thing. I'd already given them nearly 20 years of my life. I made my way through the ranks and the most elite assignments. As an investigative analyst with the Drug Enforcement Administration, I got to work on some pretty cool assignments—wiretaps, legally making cocaine in South America with real-life cocaine manufacturers for government research projects, American embassy assignments abroad … blah, blah, blah. I even built a drug case against a few known government officials.

It was a pretty cool career, but I was living it at the expense of MY freedom. That realization in my spirit would not let me sleep two hours straight without wondering how I was going to redefine success without a blueprint to go by.

The urge to leave began nagging at my heart and soul. I would sit in my car for 30 minutes trying to center myself before going into the federal building in downtown Atlanta and falling in line formation with a culture of corporate workplace robots. The voice in my spirit that was once a tingle and whisper became a sledgehammer and a shout, but I wondered day and night if I could really leave or if I'd be a government robot for the rest of my life.

Through this process, my Million Dollar Identity began to unfold.

I remember five or six years earlier, I'd listened to Tony Robbins daily on my 1st generation iPod on the hour-long bus ride to work. I'd drop my son, Dylan, off to daycare each morning and race to catch the last bus going downtown. Tony always talked about mindset and choices and how you could create your reality. At the time, that seemed so far off. That was for someone else … After all, I was already successful.

But I wasn't.

Not by MY standards. By the world's standards.

I had to decide that I could redefine what success means to me ... even without a blueprint.

I could CREATE it.

I HAD to create it.

I GET to create it.

I found myself worrying about what people would think of my decision. What if I left my secure job and had to go back because things didn't work out, or what if I couldn't go back if I needed to? But it got to a point where none of that mattered.

I had to CREATE the life I wanted.

Although AJ wanted me to step into a world of entrepreneurship, he now admits he never thought I actually would.

But I did.

In January 2013, I emailed my boss with a resignation letter that I'd written in my head 1,000 times. I didn't want management to think my letter was a chess move response to my remote working request denial. That denial was just the pinnacle of realizing that I wasn't living a life I loved. I was following the world's view of success. The "NO" shook me up enough to see it more clearly than I ever had.

I wanted to have a life of freedom and choice. I wanted a life where I could be more present with my then four-year-old, Collin; my six-year-old, Dylan; and my daughter, Kelly, who was in college.

About two years before this all happened, I had started a hobby centered around natural hair and fashion. The brand grew from my basement to a multi-million-dollar brick-and-mortar fashion boutique in north Atlanta with nearly one million fans on our social media channels collectively.

I became ruthless at creating a life, business, and personal existence without walls or ceilings because I had existed so long in an environment that told me what to do, how to do it, and when to do it.

The mentality I adapted to create the life I wanted became my mantra and has allowed me to live in a Million Dollar Identity state of mind.

Within a few years of operating as a full-time entrepreneur who grew a wildly successful and world-known fashion brand, I began to get tons of emails, DMs, and inbox inquiries from all over the world about HOW I grew my brand so quickly.

People wanted to know how I had the courage to leave a successful career and how I was so confident, and they wished they could do the same. Through answering their questions, I discovered that my true passion wasn't in helping people LOOK good. It was in helping people BE and BECOME good—the highest version of themselves, aside from building a business.

As time went on, I began to feel that familiar tug again that God was preparing me for something more.

My Divine Assignment was on the horizon and unfolding by the day.

What I now know to be 100% true is that once you become the person who knows who they are, whose they are, and find confidence in that space, you are ultimately positioned to do anything in life you want. I call it stepping into your Divine Assignment.

We all have one.

Realizing this is the key to unlocking your Million Dollar Identity.

I decided it was time to again create the life I wanted. I stepped out of the world of fashion and into the world of changing lives.

I got my coaching certification with a concentration in business. I'd launched a whole multi-million-dollar brand, so I was quite comfortable with branding, marketing, building an audience, and attracting people to a common cause.

I've since become a Master Certified Life & Business Coach/Consultant. I'm also an Executive Coach to high-level entrepreneurs and leaders of Fortune 500 companies. I've coached thousands of people over the years on an array of life and business-related topics.

During the beginning of the pandemic, my calendar of clients was overloaded with people who needed a life coach to help them sort through all the emotions and turmoil of job loss, death, virtual school, and all the unforeseeable things that became inevitable results of COVID-19. I was up to my eyeballs in client meetings. I knew there had to be a better way. I just didn't know what it was yet.

I identified almost instantly that there was going to be a strong need for life coaches to support the current state of affairs. I decided to write an e-book called *How to Become a Life Coach in 2020*. I presold the idea of the book before I actually wrote the book. Preselling your book, course, or program is one way to truly vet your idea before spending tons of time creating what you think your audience needs instead of just asking them.

All the constantly unfolding shenanigans of virtual school with a 10- and 12-year-old didn't allow me much time to write an e-book. Feeding folks, washing laundry, and scouring the grocery store aisles for tissue were keeping my focus.

The day before the book was set to release, I decided to teach the same content in a live workshop instead of publishing an e-book. I put together a quick landing page and emailed my list. Within less than a week, over 500 people registered for the workshop. I was blown away but knew I was onto something great.

I've been in the marketing industry long enough to know that only 20% to 30% of people actually show up for free workshops and master-classes, and even less actually enroll into the paid program typically offered at the end.

I had to remind myself that there are no walls or ceilings ... Just go and let it all unfold.

Within a week, I'd hosted the workshop, and a little over 100 people attended live. A whopping 53 people enrolled in a group coaching program! I called it the Life Coach 30-Day Bootcamp. I have since renamed it the Impactful & Paid Coach Bootcamp.

Here's the thing ... I had no content created for the program. I knew the transformation I could facilitate was to teach an "everyday" person the skill set and the business of coaching. I knew I could do it in a 30-day Bootcamp-style container, so I did.

The program was set to begin a few days later. I quickly created a Facebook group and a few mindset videos that should be at the beginning of all programs. I soon discovered that the word was out and more people wanted another workshop.

The fact that I know that we get to create life and business to be anything we want, plus the fact that I was operating in my Divine Assignment, gave me the confidence and courage to roll out the first cohort of 53 people while also advertising another workshop.

By week two of the Cohort 1 Bootcamp (we call them my "Day Ones" in my community), they were so intrigued that they didn't want the 30 days to end. I knew I needed to create a next-level program.

The secret is that I closely watched their Facebook support group, interacted with them there daily, used the feedback from the mindset videos, layered it with the transformation of becoming a life coach, and created each day's content a day or two ahead of them.

So, when they were watching Day 5 in their Kajabi member portal, I was creating Day 7. When they were on Day 7, I'd create the video training for Day 9 and upload it to their portal. They had no idea. They only knew that the next day of their training would be available at 10 a.m. each morning.

There were days where it was uploaded moments before the automated email would be distributed by the system, advising them their next training class was ready.

I'll be honest and share; it was A LOT OF WORK. But once you create the 30 days of Bootcamp content, you have an asset that will pay you repeatedly. And the other beautiful thing is that the daily content provides the training to support the transformative result.

The framework, which I now teach to other coaches, only requires you to show up live once weekly for the 30 days for live Q & A relevant to course content. This allows you to host a weekly class from anywhere because you are not teaching; you're answering questions for one hour.

By week three, I hosted a second workshop and offered the opportunity to be in the Bootcamp Cohort 2. I also dropped a teaser for Bootcamp Cohort 1, letting them know that I was launching an 8-week Mentorship & Certification course available to a few people after the Bootcamp was over. The investment for this was significantly higher than they'd paid for the initial Bootcamp.

Sixteen people enrolled in my first group coaching high-ticket program.

I've previously sold high-ticket but only to individuals. I was under the belief that no one would pay me a four- or five-figure amount to join a program with other people. Right?

WRONG.

I look back now and know that small thinking mindset gremlins were playing tricks on my belief. It happens to the best of us as our Million Dollar Identity unfolds internally.

I suppose I knew deep down inside it was possible because, by that time, I'd paid a high-ticket investment to attend several Tony Robbins events, including $10K to attend his well-known Business Mastery One in Las Vegas and $15K for Business Mastery Two in the Netherlands. And AJ and I both attended.

I had also been in several Inner Circles, including Leadership Boardroom and Frank Kern's Inner Circle. At that point, I'd spent $150K+ in my personal business development training.

I discovered that what you identify as a hurdle is a hurdle indeed. The only reason I had not previously enrolled people into a group high-ticket coaching program is that I didn't have one for them to enroll in.

Since then, I have built an ecosystem in my business where I host workshops and upsell at the end into a 30-day Bootcamp experience. At the end of the 30 days, I provide an opportunity for them to enroll in a high-ticket program where I teach them how to build the exact same machine I built that now allows me to work less than I ever have and make more than I've ever made.

Can you imagine if you created a coaching program that positively impacted so many people and you only had to provide live support four hours each month?

Wouldn't it be awesome if you could host those four Zoom calls from anywhere in the world because you went ALL IN on 30 days of creating a program that will generate income over and over and over again?

Did you realize you could launch your first or next high-ticket program in the next 30 days on the backend of your very own Bootcamp-style coaching program centered around one main transformation that your audience already wants and needs?

Did I mention that the people in the Bootcamp who were not ready and/or able to invest in the high-ticket program were filtered into an ongoing membership program, and the only deliverable is a monthly meeting that is hosted by one of the Client Success Coaches on my staff?

From April to December 2020, I taught four live workshops and sold the 30-day Bootcamp coaching program at the end of it and generated at least five figures in each launch.

At the end of each 30 days of the Bootcamp-style coaching program, I sold the high-ticket group coaching program. I created at least five figures each time I did that. This allowed me to have seven 5-figure launches during the peak of the pandemic.

Since then, I have used the same workshop to promote the 30-day Bootcamp and have had a few $100K days and a $250K month in November 2021.

My Million Dollar Identity expanded as I began to facilitate deep transformations that the supportive environment of group coaching programs foster.

The thing I love the most in all of this is I now get to teach coaches how to create group coaching programs of their own. That is the ecosystem I built during the height of the pandemic that has quickly become the blueprint that teaches others.

I am no longer a corporate career robot. I CREATE the life I want daily and teach other coaches to do the same.

Part of stepping into your Million Dollar Identity is realizing that you can create the life you want, too. All you have to do is decide.

Group coaching changed my life. It expanded my reach and quantum leaped my authority in the coaching space because I developed the blueprint that can allow you to work less and increase your impact, influence, and income.

Group coaching is the only way you are truly able to grow and scale your business while working less and generating more.

If you're ready to step into your Million Dollar Identity, grab my e-book, 5-Figure Launches on Demand—The Group Coaching Blueprint. My team and I can help guide and support you in building the group coaching ecosystem in your business.

As coaches, we are vessels to the transformation of many. Take that on as your identity, your mission … your Divine Assignment.

To find out more, visit my website at:

CoachKellyJ.com

CHAPTER TEN

TERESA HARDING

Teresa Harding

Teresa Harding built her first successful business in dōTERRA, which grew to over a billion dollars in sales in 8.5 years and is still going strong. She is a Founding Presidential Diamond in the company and has a team of over five million Wellness Advocates. She is invited to speak and train all over the world. Her business has taken her to over 60 countries worldwide, and she has been on the ground helping to open over 60 countries worldwide.

Teresa is now heavily involved in helping high net worth individuals invest in real estate. Her niche is mobile home parks and storage units. She is a master negotiator and creates incredible deals for her clients, including pocket deals that the public would never see. She finds her passion in helping people get their passive income higher than their working income.

She is married to the man she calls her "knight in shining armor," Dr. Roger Harding. They have three amazing sons who have married women who became the daughters they never had, and their children bring her so much joy. Her family has always been, and always will be, her most important priority.

FROM LYING AND STEALING TO BUILDING A BILLION-DOLLAR BUSINESS WITH INTEGRITY

"Teresa, we're calling the police and pressing charges."

This was the moment that scared me more than anything I'd heard, ever! And I didn't know it then, but it would become one of the defining moments in my entrepreneurial journey.

I thought I was too smart to get caught. But let's back up ...

I wasn't always a liar and a thief. I started out like any other kid. But somewhere along the way, I figured out that by lying and stealing, I could get pretty much anything I wanted (or at least what I thought I wanted).

And the sad part is, I got really good at it. I figured out a system to steal money from the till at Burger King when I was working there. I figured out how to manipulate the numbers to con the newspaper company I was working for so that I would win the grand prize—the sweetest bike I had ever seen.

In school, all I really wanted was to be liked. I wanted to have friends and I didn't have a single one. I felt sorry for myself and focused on it all the time.

We had a big family, and times were tough, so my parents didn't have the money to buy me the shoes and clothes and "stuff" that I thought would make me cool. I thought that was why I didn't have friends.

The next several years were rough. In high school, I was still playing my con games. My family couldn't trust me and didn't believe anything I said, but I still thought this was the best way to get what I wanted and fulfill what I thought were my dreams. I still wondered why I didn't have any friends and why life was never fair. Why did all the good things happen to other people?

My lying and stealing went on and on. I thought I was invincible and that everyone around me was an idiot. I knew I'd never get caught!

Until one day, I did. I was stealing from a local market and they caught me red-handed. They sat me on a stool and said words to me that I wouldn't wish on my worst enemy.

"We're calling the police and pressing charges!"

They said they had called my parents who were on their way over. It was the first time I remember being truly scared. It was the first time I remember feeling like I was actually going to have legitimate consequences for my behavior. My young life literally flashed before my eyes, and I knew I was going to prison.

My parents showed up and they were livid. I was truly scared of what was going to happen, but this time, it was the good kind of scared. The kind that made me start to humble myself and realize I couldn't keep going like this. It was the first time I EVER remember feeling that feeling.

Then my parents made a serious mistake. At the end of the yelling lecture, they said these words, "You're lucky these people are our friends or they'd be calling the police!"

Wait! WHAT? So they hadn't called the police yet? Ooookaaaay. My heart immediately switched from "Oh no, I've finally gone too far" to

"Oh, wow. These adults are such idiots! I can do whatever I want and they will never be able to keep up. Ha ha. I've got this down." No more fear, no more guilt. I squashed the little light inside of me that had tried to push through and help me.

Things didn't change for me until I observed something that changed the direction my life was going. I still remember the feeling that day, this deep and powerful knowledge inside, that God was making sure this hit me on the head. Of course, back then, I didn't know that it would not only change who I was and who I would become, but it would even be the thing that made me a very successful entrepreneur. It would help me turn a start-up business into a billion-dollar business. And I would do it all with a very high level of honesty and integrity.

What I saw that day all happened because of my older sister, Julienne. Some of us had gone to support her at one of her events at school. I watched as she arrived and started circling the room, talking with different groups of her peers. She talked with the group of kids that were considered the druggies, she joked with her group of Mexican friends, she laughed with the popular kids, she loved on the group everyone called Gothic. She couldn't walk two steps without someone wanting to hug her, talk to her, or interact with her.

And as I watched, I remember thinking what I always thought, "Why doesn't everybody like me like that? Why don't I have friends like that? It's not fair because I'm as cool as her; people just don't see it." But then, as I watched, I noticed something profound that I had never paid attention to before.

She made every person in that whole event feel like it was all about them. She cared about them, she was excited to see them, she wanted to know about them. It was obvious that none of this was the least bit about her. She wasn't thinking about herself or what she could get out of it.

That hit me really hard. In a shameful, humbling, seeing who I really was kind of hard. But that's not even what hit me the hardest.

I saw the look of utter love and loyalty in their eyes, and something inside me changed! Maybe it's because that's what I'd always wanted— for people to treat me that way and love me that way.

Something inside my brain clicked that day, and I realized for the first time that I had been looking at everything inside out and upside down. How had I gotten it so wrong?

I realized I wanted to create that feeling for other people. It was the first time in my life I ever remember having a plan that wasn't self-serving.

The crazy thing is that when I stopped thinking about what I wanted or what was in it for me and spent my whole focus on how to help other people get what they desired, I started getting everything I desired and more, without even trying or thinking about it.

My life changed so fast that it was almost miraculous. I was voted in by the student body as princess for the school court the following year, my junior year. I was literally shocked! I didn't know my reputation had changed. Then in my senior year, I was crowned queen of the court, the most prestigious position possible. It was an honor I'll never forget because it felt like people were sending a message of approval.

Over the next several years, I tried my hand at sales and some of my own businesses. I sold "free" insulation door to door for the electric company in California. I bred dogs, I sold kitchen tools, I even got into real estate as the middle man between the owner of a property going into foreclosure and a potential buyer.

I got married, and when we started having children, I knew I wanted to be the one who raised them. I wanted the influence in their life to be me, not a babysitter, so from the time they were born, I was a stay-at-home mom. It was the hardest transition for me to go from working to being at home because I was so driven in business, but it was the best decision I've ever made.

We had three boys, and when they were in high school, I was introduced to essential oils by a start-up company called dōTERRA. The oils were extremely high quality and could be used for health and medicinal purposes. I was extremely skeptical until I saw them help with my three-year-old niece, Lacey.

Lacey was fine one day, and the next, she started having these episodes where her whole body would begin to shake. Within three days, she was having eight to 15 of these episodes a day.

Lacey had to take medications to help stop the episodes but they all had side effects. One of them made her behave as if she were drunk. She would slur her words and she couldn't walk more than a couple of steps without falling down. She would get so frustrated.

They only lived a few blocks from me, so sometimes I would babysit Lacey. You couldn't even let her sit on a chair by herself because if one of her episodes started, she could fall off. This had all been going on for about three months when a friend of my sister's told her, "You should try frankincense essential oil." I thought, "Ohhhh, brother! Are you kidding me? Like that's going to help."

But when you've tried everything and nothing is working, you've got to do something. My sister tried the frankincense, and Lacey's episodes stopped that day! I couldn't believe it. I was living it with my sister, so I knew it was real. I wanted to understand how it worked, so I started doing research.

I found that one of the compounds naturally found in frankincense is alpha-pinene. Alpha-pinenes are known as the most powerful compounds to help with the inflammation that causes irritation in the body. From researching Lacey's episodes, I knew that inflammation was one of the main causes of them, so this was something I could wrap my head around.

I started using it for my own family. I had what seemed like miraculous experiences with them, so I started sharing the oils with other people because I wanted to help them. Did you get that connection? *Because I wanted to help them.* I wasn't thinking about what was in it for me.

I ended up starting a business selling those oils. I started in 2008 and I remember thinking, "Man, when I get to the point where I am making an extra $1,000 a month it's going to change our lives."

It actually turned into a business where people were buying from me and my team from all over the United States. Then we started getting sales from other countries. I would travel internationally to help open those new markets. My company was selling millions and millions of dollars of product every month, and it just kept growing bigger. My business turned into a billion-dollar company in eight and a half years.

Because I had become so successful, other people wanted me to train them. I was being invited all over the world to teach about health and to train on business and sales. I realized we had created a powerful sales process that worked no matter who we were talking to.

I believe that good training will help a lot of people, and my training has become brilliant! And don't think for one second it was because I was brilliant. I'm definitely not! My training was brilliant because I had made more mistakes than anyone I had ever seen in this business. And I had the privilege of working with a lot of amazing people, and we learned a lot from each other. That training was made up of what all of us had learned together. I had just figured out that my superpower was putting it all together in what I call *Step Skipping Strategies.*

Step Skipping Strategies is what I want to help you with. The people who came before you had to figure out things the hard way! If you can trust someone who has already accomplished what you are trying to achieve, then you will have the advantage of taking what I'm telling you and incorporating it into what you do in your business.

I have trained hundreds of thousands of people all over the world, and I love helping them get the results they're looking for. But do you know what we inevitably spend about 80 percent of our time on? Helping them *become* something different. Helping them change the habits and behaviors that are blocking their success.

Learning Discipline

Jim Rohn says, "Discipline is how to capture the emotion and turn it into equity." What he meant is that every single time we take action because we have an emotion, every time we feel inspired and we do the thing, it turns into more power inside of us. More power to go after what we want. More power to make better decisions every time we encounter a corridor of consequence, which is a decision that will be consequential in your life.

Let's be honest. It takes discipline to act, and discipline isn't a very sexy word! But discipline is actually very exciting because every time you choose to act, every time you set up a discipline to follow through with something you want to do, your action muscles get stronger. And every time your action muscles get stronger, it gets easier to do it the next time.

When you decide you're going to be on time and you discipline yourself to take that action, the next time, it's easier. If you get up and get your day started when you said you were going to, it's easier the next time. Reading that book you said you were going to read, spending that time with your family that you said you were going to spend. Everything you do affects everything else.

We've all seen people who say they want to build a business and create something that will change people's lives. But then, over time, they give up a little bit on their dream here and then a little bit there, until pretty soon they say that's not really what they wanted anyway. You've seen people do this with losing weight, personal habits, and their health.

It's true that over time as our perspective in life changes, our dreams and our vision will change, but check yourself to make sure your vision and your dream didn't change because you slowly let your lack of discipline erode away what you wanted for your life. If you find yourself thinking, well, I've just discovered that what I always wanted isn't really possible, that's a huge red flag that you have fallen prey to this debilitating change of philosophy.

But the great thing about this is the reverse is also true. Every little discipline you do, every little action you take will inspire you to do the next action, and that will inspire you to do the next and the next. It will build on itself. In my experience, the disciplines that build on themselves actually work faster to build you up. I believe the reason for this is because when you take action and follow through with that discipline, there's an excitement and a fulfilling emotion that comes along with it that inspires you to the next action.

Taking Action

Taking action comes down to two things. Number one is discipline, and number two is practice and skill.

Not taking action can cause you to miss out on some of life's best opportunities. When you have the opportunity to pull the trigger, you don't. Whatever is stopping you denies you the right to have the consequences you want. You might not take action because you are afraid of a real and present danger, concerned about a possible future failure, or feel like you need to gather more information.

But the bottom line is, you are not taking action. You are missing the moment of execution. You have come across a corridor of consequence, and rather than take action, you wait.

Every one of us has missed out on an opportunity because we didn't take action. Is that bad or good? It's only bad if you didn't choose because you didn't recognize you had a choice or because you were too afraid to grasp what life was handing you.

So the next question is, is it too late to be able to have the opportunity I missed out on? Will I get that opportunity again? The answer is no, and yes! You may have missed out on opportunities in the past, and no, those exact opportunities are not coming back (except on very rare occasions). But life works in a cycle. The cycle of corridors of consequence comes back again and again.

Every time you encounter a new corridor of consequence, you get another opportunity to practice. The only thing that matters is that you get better at it, so with the next opportunity you make better choices, which will eventually get you to a place where you are able to pick and choose exactly what you want to take from each corridor of consequence. But you have to be prepared to take action.

We all get excited to take action. But studies show us that only 1% to 3% of us actually take the action, and even fewer do it consistently. But that doesn't have to be you. What you need to do is practice the skill of taking action until you build that kind of character. The way you practice that skill is that you take action at the moment when the feeling is high and the idea is hot! The more you do this, the easier it becomes.

You will quickly get to a place where making a decision is easy for you. When you start making quicker decisions, you may sometimes make the wrong one. But guess what, making decisions too slowly is also causing you to make the wrong ones. You've practiced making slow decisions or not making decisions for whatever reason, so now it's time to practice making that decision and taking action.

So if your life is not where you want it to be right now, if the consequences you are experiencing are not the ones you have in mind for yourself, the whole key to reversing that process is to start adding one discipline at a time. The easiest way to do that is to act on the idea of the moment. When you have that ah-ha moment, when you feel inspired about going in a certain direction with your business or with your life, act on that right now. And if you want some help getting started from someone who has lots of practice, visit me here, and let's change things for you once and for all!

TeresaHarding.com/PassiveIncomeGenerator

CHAPTER ELEVEN

THE KITTI SISTERS

The Kitti Sisters

Palmy and Nancy Kitti, a sister duo team obsessed with all things financial freedom, passive income, and apartment investing, turned a $2,000 bank account into an eight-figure empire. They are apartment syndication experts, passive income crusaders, data crunchers, self-care activists, and world travelers. To date, they've helped thousands of investors scale their portfolios through apartment syndication in order to live their lifestyle dreams and reclaim their most valuable resource: *Time.*

FIND FINANCIAL FREEDOM WITH PASSIVE INCOME

There's nothing like living a life you think you're meant to be living, only to have it all ripped away.

We've been there.

We can both still remember it like it was yesterday—we were working in the fashion industry, and we loved it. We were thriving in fashion manufacturing careers.

But then, overnight, our biggest client announced that they were shutting down all of their retail stores. We will never forget the feeling of losing 90% of our income in one day. Our financial security was gone.

And so were we. Kicked to the curb.

We didn't know what we were going to do. We had been living the typical American dream. We were making good money and living life.

That is, until we didn't have that career anymore.

While we both had some savings to fall back on, we certainly didn't have enough to keep living the lives we had designed.

We would find ourselves waking up in the middle of the night, drenched in an icy cold sweat, watching our future slip away. We had no idea how we would live out our dreams. Or support our families. Or ourselves.

We only had that one source of income, and living without it made us realize how tenuous that foundation was that we'd built our lifestyles on.

Maybe you've felt those 2 a.m. night sweats, too. Maybe you've woken up in the middle of the night in utter panic about how on earth you were going to pay for your kid's college, pay off your house, or simply live your life.

Here's the thing; you're not meant to live this life where all of your finances are dependent on one source of income. That's what we had been doing because we thought that was the way of life. The American dream. The best of the best.

And that's what so many of us are taught. Go to college. Get a full-time job. Work 40 hours a week (maybe more like 60). Save an emergency fund. Put some cash in an IRA. Retire.

The so-called "American Dream."

But, what no one tells you is that doing all that isn't going to get you to the dream life you want to live. Contributing to a retirement fund or to social security is seldom enough to retire comfortably, no matter what other people tell you.

We realized this the hard way. Because, by all accounts, we'd done everything right. We had gotten full-time jobs, we had worked hard at them, and we had built careers.

But everything came to a screeching halt when that one client of ours shut down their retail stores. The truth glared back at us that the "right" thing wasn't the right thing at all. The lives we wanted to live— the ones of complete freedom and fulfillment—weren't happening with our one source of income and full-time jobs. We needed something bigger and better.

However, finding that bigger and better thing was also harder than it looked. When we started researching investment opportunities and ways to diversify our income, we were gobsmacked by the amount of finance nonsense all over the internet—pretty much designed to make investing and financial freedom impossible to get involved in and understand unless you were a hedge fund manager or Leo DiCaprio's character in *Wolf of Wall Street*.

No thanks.

Instead of finding easy-to-understand advice, we were consistently greeted with high barriers to entry and a lack of viable opportunities. Everything seemed more complicated than it really was. Most of the financial advice around investing made it seem like we needed to be billionaires to start, and most of the people we met were not welcoming us into the investment club.

We threw ourselves into learning everything we could about investing and ways to have financial freedom. We went down several paths including house flipping, but even though we were good at it, we quickly realized that we were still trading our time for money.

We kept on researching and finally discovered our big kahuna—the one thing that has let us grow our wealth and help other investors grow their wealth. But it wasn't one of the main things people typically talk about when it comes to investing.

It wasn't the stock market.

It wasn't cryptocurrency.

And it wasn't real estate.

Well, it was actually a specialized branch of real estate—a niche that most people have never even heard of. We certainly hadn't.

Once we became obsessed with all things financial freedom and passive income, we finally discovered apartment investing and managed to turn a $2,000 bank account into an eight-figure empire.

The answer we had been searching for was apartment syndication—specifically, multifamily apartment syndication. And when we found it, those 2 a.m. night sweats stopped.

It wasn't long before we started raking in big profits with apartment investing for us and for our passive investors, and we became addicted to the game.

To the selection.

To the freedom.

To the life.

We FINALLY started living the lives we were meant to live, not just the lives we thought we were meant to live.

After getting to play this game, enjoy this freedom, and live this life, we realized almost instantly that there was nothing either of us wanted to do more than to help other people learn how to do the same.

Once we started talking to people, we realized what their BIGGEST fears were: stressing about retirement, putting kids through college, worrying about being a burden to family members at an old age, being afraid to see wealth wash away in an economic downturn, and being scared of losing their job.

Your Ticket to Financial Freedom

Financial freedom is really and genuinely not made up of tiny decisions, like choosing whether or not to buy the $7 latte. Financial freedom is really and genuinely made up of big decisions—$50K decisions, $1 million decisions.

That's why apartment syndication and apartment investing are so powerful—because working with investment experts can be your answer to every single worry and anxiety about money that you have.

Apartment and real estate investing, as a whole, has a few potential entry points, from buying a property outright to investing with a REIT to apartment syndication investment opportunities. Multifamily apartment syndication, however, allows you to go in with a group of investors to purchase an apartment building without the need to be a landlord.

With apartment syndication, the investment is lower than many other forms of real estate investing, but the profits aren't. Plus, multifamily apartment investing can get you involved in the commercial real estate game in ways you may not have been able to afford. There are massive tax benefits, too, and, more than anything, apartment syndication is COMPLETELY passive.

Understanding Apartment Syndication Investing

In multifamily apartment syndication, there are two main roles: the general partner or syndicator, and the passive investors. The general partner or syndicator is the one who has to deal with all of the big stuff. Their job is to find the building, secure the investment, do all the paperwork, and deal with the landlord-y things like finding a property management company to correspond with the tenants.

However, passive investors just have one job: to invest. And then, all they have to do is sit back and enjoy the cash flow, profits, and massive tax benefits.

Multifamily apartment syndication investing is widely seen as the area of investment that can get you the highest return on investment. Typically, multifamily investors can expect up to an average total return of anywhere from 80% to 100%, with half of that coming back to them each month/quarter through apartment cash flow (rent, pet fees, deposits, etc.), and half of that coming from the eventual sale of the property.

While not every deal is exactly five years, five years allows our team to best exit a property at a certain time if the market is peaking, or hold to move through a low point in the market. Five years also gives us the time to execute the business plan for renovations, the unit turns, and add value to the property, thereby increasing income—which means that most of our apartment investors see that return just a few years after making their initial investments.

Plus, here's the real secret; passive income is, absolutely, the key to reaching true wealth and financial freedom. When you can passively bring in the amount of money that allows you to live your dream life—without clocking into work every single day, in and out, from 9–5—you've achieved financial freedom.

Apartment syndication helps you achieve that.

This is super important, too, because it is better than other types of investments. For example, the average stock market return for the last 15 years has been close to 7.04%. Then, once you take fees, taxes, and inflation into account, it gets closer to 2.5%. With compounding interest and growing properties, passive investors in apartments are regularly receiving above-average returns.

They keep rolling and recycling their investments into more deals, more cash flow, and more passive income streams. And then they get rich and get to do whatever they want, like spending their life drinking mai tais on a beach in Bali, while cash flow keeps getting deposited into their accounts.

The way we see it, THAT is the true American dream. When you pair it with tax savings and additional financial benefits, you literally cannot go wrong. While there is always going to be some risk with investment opportunities, real estate tends to carry a lower risk, as everyone needs a place to live, no matter what the economic environment looks like.

Our passive investors also see massive tax benefits due to what is called "bonus depreciation"; their investment income is taxed at a much lower rate than other investments.

The best part of apartment investing is that it requires little to no time investment, which means true time freedom. For most people, the real American dream means having enough money to live life without worrying about the day-to-day. To spend time with loved ones. To retire when they want.

Let's be honest: The "American Dream" is antiquated. It's not a thing anymore. People can't just save a couple of dollars each month, build that house with the white picket fence, and have enough money to retire.

The REAL American dream is one that you create. Maybe it does mean you want a white picket fence and a minivan (and that's okay).

But it's why we are such huge fans of getting people involved in passive investments when and wherever they can—because passive income and passive investing can actually get them to that dream.

More importantly, though? It lets you define your own American dream.

There's nothing better than defining your dream, your life, your freedom. And for us, it's thrilling to be able to be part of helping to change people's lives. We can't even explain how amazing it feels!

Our mission is simple. We are the solution for giving you PEACE. We're not about chasing deals—or losing money (yours OR ours). As economic experts and experienced investors, we walk both sides of the investment table as both general and limited partners. We obsessively vet deals and analyze each step, and we have a proven track record of full-cycle deals that give our investors opportunities to get a return on their investments in five years or less.

Our portfolio is huge, our investor pool is connected, and our purposes are strong. You see, we're about "making more while doing less (for real)."

We have a lot of people ask about entering as an apartment investor, although most people think that this type of real estate investing requires a Bruce Wayne level of income to start. In fact, our investors can start with initial investments of $50K. A lot of money, yes, but nothing unheard of—especially in real estate.

Unlike other gurus, we don't believe that money is made during the buying process, but rather when you implement and execute the right business plans. While single-family home values are based on comparables, apartment values are based on the value of net operating income divided by cap rate, meaning it's based on how much income you can produce in each property.

We don't advocate fixed interest rate loans; instead, we like using a floater interest rate loan with an interest rate cap, otherwise, there's no flexibility when we want to exit (sell) the apartment building. When we use a floater interest rate, we're not subjected to a prepayment penalty, which could be millions of dollars.

You see, while other general partners have a holding period of ten years, we love models of five years or less. We understand that wealth has the need for speed. Our investment opportunities have an average hold period of 23.5 months. When the properties hit the projected returns, our philosophy is to sell right away, because we truly understand what our investors want, which is the quickest path to wealth.

And at the heart, we are still very active passive-investors in other apartment syndications. While we get the thrill of being general partners, we love to also make money while we sleep. See, when we are active passive-investors, we also look at things from a passive investors' side and would not present our investors with an investment opportunity that we wouldn't put our money in.

There is no other kind of investing that consistently gets these kinds of returns when going all-in—no other kind. Not even close.

You don't have to invest a zillion dollars.

You don't have to wait 50 years to see a return.

You're not at the mercy of a volatile stock market.

You don't need to take on extra responsibilities or spend extra time.

You get to choose what you invest in.

So, let's play a quick game:

Option 1: You keep your savings in a savings account. That money may grow a little—likely by a couple of dollars (however, you'll likely lose out big-time to inflation).

Option 2: You can try out some stocks or something like Bitcoin, a fun but volatile asset that takes a while to see a return on.

Option 3: You can go the typical way, contributing to your employer's retirement plan, maybe eventually having enough to retire … though you're probably not going to be living as fun of a life as you could.

Option 4: You can create a passive income stream through apartment syndication investments that gives you true financial freedom without waiting years and years and years. In fact, you'd see an ROI in right around five years, maybe less.

Which one do you want?

If you chose Option 4, we can help!

To date, we've helped thousands of investors secure their financial futures while paying virtually $0 taxes via apartment syndication (legally, ethically, and morally, of course!). We've saved over $30 million in taxes, and have apartment investment opportunities go full cycle (AKA, SOLD!) in an average of 23.5 months.

In our investor's group, The Kitti Freedom Club, we choose apartment properties that make sense. We work to maximize loan proceeds by using flexible terms so that our investors can make more money, as opposed to sticking to things like fixed interest rates.

We also focus on investing in landlord-friendly markets with above-average cap rates and focus on those with a high population, job, and organic rent growth—think Texas, Arizona, Georgia, etc. By investing in markets with multiple economic drivers, such as oil, tech, medical, financial services, manufacturing, and aerospace—as opposed to just one—we're able to better ensure higher returns.

We believe in the transformative power of money (and transformative, it is)! Not only that, but we believe in the velocity of money and the way it can continue to grow within itself to reach high levels of excellence. We're not your average investor team (heck, not even close), and we're not a stuffy one, either. In the Kitti Freedom Club, we create wealthy people in a fraction of the time.

And we'd love to have you join us. You can go from not knowing whom to trust to knowing where to invest, what the exact numbers are that we track to see what's working (and what's not!), and how to refine your strategy going forward with our step-by-step Apartment Syndication System.

By approaching investing with a strategic eye (and genuine love and care for our investors), we're able to strike a unique balance between relationship building and wealth building. What is even close to better than that?

So, if you're ready to finally live that freedom-filled life of your dreams, we're ready for you, too. Come find us, invest with us, and grow your wealth and your portfolio with tax-advantaged, strategic, smart investments.

TheKittiSisters.com

CHAPTER TWELVE

GALEN M. HAIR

Galen M. Hair

Galen M. Hair is a litigator at Insurance Claim HQ. He is licensed in multiple states and boasts clients from around the world. With large wins both at home and across the country, Mr. Hair focuses not only on the current litigation the client is facing but also on the long-term personal and business issues that might be affected.

Mr. Hair combines a comprehensive large firm approach with a small boutique firm model to achieve impressive results with minimal expense. This unwavering success to continual improvement has led him to be named as a Super Lawyer Rising Star, a Top Lawyer by *New Orleans Magazine*, and to receive the Pro Bono Publico Award and numerous other accolades.

TURNING TRAGEDY
INTO POSSIBILITY

Hurricane Katrina changed the trajectory of my life forever. I was a college student at the time, studying to be an opera singer. I heard about the devastation in New Orleans, so I headed down there to see if I could help out. Frankly, I wasn't good for much other than offering physical labor. But as I was working, I listened to the conversations going on around me with law students and lawyers. It was eye-opening for me, and I had this ah-ha moment when I decided that I wanted to go into the legal field.

When I graduated from law school, I was offered a huge salary to work for a defense firm in New York. I grew up with a single mom and we were poor, I mean the kind of poor where you don't know how you are going to pay the next electric bill to keep the lights on. So for me, they dangled the money carrot and I bit.

Fast forward several years; I was representing an energy company that refused to pay claims to a group of businesses that had had their buildings burned down. Our firm's job was to deny or underpay the businesses' claims.

I had had some twinges of conscience before this and was starting to think that I had lost my way in terms of who I was and wanted to be in the world. I had a turning point in my law career during that case when the widow of one of the families looked deep into my eyes and told me just where I could go! Her choice words hit home. We were sentencing this woman to financial hardship for the rest of her life because it was our job as the lawyers representing the insurance company to deny or underpay the claims.

That's when I had what I call my Jerry Maguire moment. What she said struck me to the core of who I am. I didn't want to be that person, so I decided to seek out other opportunities. I reached out to a good friend from law school who had started his firm. He and my best friend were working together, and the three of us decided to start our practice.

We started helping claimants hold insurance companies accountable. I felt like I had found my purpose in life, and I have never looked back.

I remember a client coming to me who was in an absolutely terrible place. He was sleeping in his car with his two kids. He had nowhere to go. His home was filled with dangerous mold. It was toxic and if they even stepped inside their house, they immediately got sick.

When I first met him, he was lost. He thought his life was over. He was worried he was going to lose his kids and he was going to end up in a homeless shelter.

He had an insurance company. You know, one of those that advertise a lot about how great they are, but they were not great. They left him high and dry. He had a little bit of retirement money saved up. He was in the process of using that money to survive, and he still was living in his car because he just knew that money wouldn't go very far.

We fought that case for two-and-a-half years. We ultimately got him enough money to build a brand new home and replenish his retirement funds.

No one will ever undo the damage that those kids must have suffered living in a car for weeks and weeks before we met them. But it felt good to help restore them to some semblance of normalcy.

People hear these stories and think that it isn't going to happen to them or that they will be alright if it does. But I see this day in and day out.

These situations lead to homelessness, loss of jobs, divorce, and even suicide as a result of not having a claim paid quickly enough.

We have several clients who lost their houses in Hurricane Laura in September 2020 and are still living in trailers. We have a client who can only live in two out of the seven rooms in her house because the other rooms are moldy and toxic. I have clients who have been living with family for several years as the result of a broken water pipe that flooded their home and the carrier does not want to pay fairly or on time.

This is the game that the insurance companies play. They drag it on intentionally. The carrier wants to push you over the edge. A lot of people don't have the fortitude to go through these major challenging events. They hope that if you get desperate enough, then maybe you will make a deal with them and they won't have to pay out as much money for the claim.

Many times you don't know when a disaster will strike, so it's so important to be prepared. For most people, their house is one of the biggest assets that they own, but they spend less time picking out a homeowners policy than they do purchasing a car.

If you are looking for a policy or want to be sure you are adequately protected, do your research. I would recommend finding an insurance agent and meeting with them versus buying a policy on the internet. Research the insurance company to see how often they are getting sued, if they have had or currently have class action suits filed against them, and if you think the allegations might be true.

If you already have insurance, get a copy of the policy and review it. Does it cover what needs to be covered on the house and property? Does it protect you against the types of perils that may hit your geographical region?

For example, I wouldn't be too worried about ice storms in Florida or earthquakes in Virginia, but you want to be sure that disasters that could happen are adequately covered so there are no hidden surprises.

It might be hard to figure out all the insurance lingo on your own, so I would advise having an insurance agent walk you through the policy to make sure that they understand the coverage you want, and you understand what you may be giving up with the policy you agree to.

Once you have a policy that you feel comfortable with, you want to think about physical protection. In the event of an upcoming disaster, you want to secure your home and protect it as much as possible from the elements.

Many times we don't know that a disaster is coming, so routine maintenance is crucial. I know it's hard to keep up with the demands of being a homeowner, but in a perfect world, you should do a monthly check of both the interior and exterior of your home, looking for areas of decay, breakage, and anything that needs to be fixed.

One of the most common areas that insurance companies use to deny a claim is what's called deferred maintenance or preexisting damage. I know it's so tempting to put off those repairs, but by regularly maintaining your house you can avoid this issue.

The last thing I can suggest is to be sure your house has the appropriate building materials for your geographic area. For example, you wouldn't want cheap windows in a hurricane region such as Louisiana.

Following some of these tips may help you when disaster strikes, but if you need more expertise, my company is very specialized. To understand how to successfully maneuver a property policy, you have to understand how construction works, how insurance works, and how contract law works. If you're deficient in any one of those categories, you're fighting with your hands tied behind your back. It's odd to me that, in this particular area, so many people think that they can handle their claim.

I have gotten to be an expert in this area because I live it every day. When I'm not in a hearing or working on a case, I'm reading. I'm following the latest trends in insurance and construction. I know what codes apply and why they apply when I'm talking about building codes. I know how they can be applied to a specific insurance policy. This isn't something I'm able to do because I'm just naturally smart but because I have a passion for it, and I've dedicated my life to making sure that policyholders are paid fairly by insurance companies.

In reality, very few companies have done that. There are a lot of people that say that they have, but when you look at the economics of it, they're not necessarily doing that. For instance, there are roofing companies that say that they specialize in insurance claims. But they don't specialize in insurance claims, they specialize in getting insurance companies to buy big roofs that they build.

Public adjusters claim that they specialize in insurance claims, but they don't. They charge a percentage of the money that you recover on the structure portion of your claim, and sometimes the contents, so they focus on those two things.

I learned how to maneuver a claim from beginning to end. Specializing in insurance claims takes time. It takes pain. It takes tears. But it's what we do. We have been successful because we are good at what we do and we have figured out how to solve these problems.

If some type of disaster comes your way, there are certain steps that those with a Million Dollar Identity take to ensure that they get fully compensated for their losses.

Step 1: Get help. You either need a qualified public adjuster or you need a qualified attorney. I know that's hard to find and Google is not your best friend, but you need to look for people who know what they're doing.

I can say this a million times, but if you're not getting help, you are already losing.

One of my business philosophies is that if you're not growing, you're dying. Insurance claims are the same. You have to actively keep moving your claim forward and attempt to reach what I call full indemnity (which is the phrase used when we are talking about getting enough funds to rebuild after a disaster minus your deductible).

Every minute that you spend doing something other than pushing that forward is ultimately time that your claim is being actively worked against you by your carrier.

Step 2: Collect information. This is important even if you get the best public adjuster attorney in the world. They need information from you. What did your house or business look like before the disaster?

You need to make a clear list of everything that you've noticed that's different now. That list may evolve, but it's important to make sure that you've collected not only a full list of what you've lost but also to be honest about what you haven't lost. Insurance fraud is rampant.

Step 3: Go over the details in your insurance policy. It is a contract and there are certain things that you have to do in that contract. Of course, it varies from contract to contract and state by state. The law may even vary, but generally speaking, you have to prepare to meet your obligations under the contract. Once the documentation is submitted, along with an evaluation of what you are owed, then it's a matter of convincing the insurance company that you are correct in your evaluation. You have to show them why you're right. We use research. We use white papers. We use meteorological data. We may use installation manuals for certain types of building materials to explain to them why something costs what it does. We use anything we can find to justify the compensation we are asking for.

Step 4: Be patient. The process takes time and it does so intentionally. Insurance companies came up with this delay, deny, and underpay system to win.

Denials are easy. You can beat a denial in court. In fact, if that denial is not well-grounded, most juries will find in your favor, since juries are not known to be pro-insurance-company.

Underpaying is a little bit harder because now you're fighting about how much money should be paid for a particular line item. But delay is the most lethal of all of them. Delay is what causes joblessness, homelessness, and divorce. It's the time, it's not really the denial.

The denial can be overturned quickly, but insurance companies delay even when you go to courts that are known for being particularly fast. Insurance companies find ways to push the hearings or the trials out in time. If you're not patient, you're setting yourself up for failure from the very beginning. But once you have the process, the process works.

If we're doing our job, our clients should be able to fully rebuild after paying their attorney fees. In many states, there's something called bad faith, which is an interesting concept. It is designed to penalize the insurance company for not behaving fairly in the adjustment of a claim. This can allow attorney fees to get reimbursed and can even allow for penalties to be paid, so one of the things we're also doing is documenting what's happening in your claim so we can explore that bad faith opportunity for you at the end.

The clients we serve who are *prepared* for disaster are the ones who rise above tragedy and make the most of opportunity. If you are struggling with an insurance claim, reach out to us with any questions you have, and we'll do our best to answer them. Also, if you go to the URL below,

I will give you a copy of my free e-book, *Overcoming Disaster*. I don't recommend that anyone handle a claim by themselves but if that is what you want to do, I recommend that you get a copy of this book. It walks you through the claims process step by step. It helps you figure out what your responsibilities are in the policy. It tells you who everyone is. It tells you who you can trust and who you might not be able to trust. Pick up your free copy here:

InsuranceClaimHQ.com/ebook

CHAPTER THIRTEEN

JAY ALTMAN

Jay Altman

Jay Altman is an Entrepreneur Success Coach and the co-owner of four successful businesses, along with his wife of 15 years, Kelly Altman. The author of multiple books and programs including *How to Grow from 6 to 7 Figures*, *Be Do Have Entrepreneur Success Coaching*, *Magic Morning*, and *Make It Rain Masterclass*, Jay has guided top-level entrepreneurs and executives to achieve their highest goals—in finance and happiness—in record time. Even though he grew up in a poor, small, farming town in northwest Indiana, he is now a self-made millionaire. Jay and Kelly currently reside in Minnesota with their four wonderful kids ranging from 3 to 15 years old.

GET CLEAR TO GET PAID

Not a day goes by that I don't think about what it felt like to lose EVERYTHING. That day is etched in my memory and has affected almost every decision I've ever made in my life and business since.

The first summer after my parents divorced, I was nine years old. My mom and I went out of town for the weekend to visit my aunt, and we drove back on the same day I had a baseball game. We stopped by our house to pick up my gear.

She pulled into the driveway and told me to run inside and grab my baseball glove that was sitting on the couch. We were in a hurry, so I ran in, but what I saw—or rather, didn't see—stopped me dead in my tracks.

Our couch was gone!

"Mom! My glove's not there! And neither is the couch!"

"Stop being stupid, get your glove, and let's go!" She was really aggravated.

"Mom, really. The couch is GONE."

She didn't believe me. But when I started to cry, she decided to get out of the car and see for herself. I followed behind her.

What we found was shocking.

Not only was our couch gone, but so were our chairs, beds, TVs, clothes, and even the meat out of the freezer!

Our house was EMPTY. We had literally lost EVERYTHING.

This kicked off a chain of events that led us to move nine times over five years. To say it was hard on our family is an understatement. But mom was resilient.

In true entrepreneurial style, my mom kept moving forward from one opportunity to the next. By the time she had started selling water filtration systems with a multi-level marketing company, I was 18 years old.

Since my parents were divorced, I went back and forth between their houses. With my dad, I lived on a farm in Indiana. Doing the daily farm chores, I knew in my heart that THIS was not my destiny.

But what I noticed was that it was common for people who lived on farms in Indiana to have sulfur water in their homes. (If you don't know what sulfur water is, consider yourself lucky because it stinks like rotten eggs and turns your clothes black in the laundry! It's pretty nasty. One of my best friend's houses had sulfur water, and I hated it.)

I saw an opportunity to join my mom in her venture to help people get better water into their homes. When I showed up at someone's house and talked to them about how clean water would change their life, I nearly always made the sale. From this job, I caught the selling bug and was motivated to sell more and keep making more and more money. It felt like freedom.

Now, not everyone loves MLMs. Some people hate them. But one thing is certain: The most successful MLMs have fantastic personal development training for their sellers.

This particular company held an annual meeting to present awards for top performers. At these meetings, not only would they talk about the exciting plans for the next year but they would also "pump up" the sellers. Their method was to bring in excellent speakers to challenge limiting beliefs and offer strategies to help each seller reach the next level in their life and business.

I attended only one of these events. The speaker that year was Tony Robbins. And the lessons I took away from that training have stuck with me ever since. Those strategies I heard as an 18-year-old kid were so powerful that I still use them today in my late 40s. These principles are the sole reason I've been able to get out of poverty and become a multimillionaire.

Tony said something like this: "If you want to be wealthy, then find somebody who is wealthy. Do what they did, and then you will get a similar result."

That's all I needed to hear. It made logical sense to me, and it seemed easy enough.

Coming out of high school, I didn't know what I wanted to do with my life, but I'd learned that it's essential to do something that you are passionate about so you can live a fulfilling life. My two passions happened to be sports and music.

I didn't know what to do with music because all I could think about was being a band director or a rock star. The rock star seemed too far-fetched, and I had no desire to be a band director.

In regard to sports, I wasn't a good enough athlete to play sports in college, let alone professionally, but I decided that if I couldn't play, I could at least train athletes to become bigger, faster, and stronger.

Based on what I had learned from Tony Robbins and the concept of modeling successful people, I got an interview with the head strength and conditioning coach at Indiana University, where I went to college.

I told him that he had my dream job, and I wanted to know how I could get that job someday. He gave me a list of certifications to get, books to read, and programs to study, etc.

I quickly started on the list, and in just a few months, I had completed it. I went back to him and asked what my next steps should be.

He said he couldn't hire me, but if I wanted to sit on a plyo-box by the wall and watch what they did in the weight room to get bigger, faster, and stronger, I could. I was ecstatic just to be in that environment, observing the techniques they used to help the players get better results.

So, I sat on the plyo-box for about six months, several days a week. When I wasn't in class, I would be on that plyo-box, watching and studying everything they were doing. I loved it!

This experience directly led to my first job in grad school as a Student Strength and Conditioning Coach.

The next step after I graduated was to get my first "real" job as the Strength and Conditioning Coach for the Minnesota Timberwolves Performance Team. I'll never forget my signing salary of $36,600. I thought I was rich! For the first time in my life, I had money to pay my rent and other living expenses.

While working as a strength coach, I was on the court at every game. I started to notice the businessmen that would occupy the "floor seats"—seats I knew were not cheap. Putting myself in that environment and being seen as an expert in my field meant that a few of these people wanted to hire me as their private trainer.

This gave me first-hand experience into how the wealthy live, how they act, and how they spend their time. One day, while training a particular client, I had a conversation that changed the way I saw the world ...

and what I believed was even possible. My client confided in me that he was upset that day because he just found out he would have to pay a six-figure tax bill!

When he told me this, all I could think about was *how in the world did you earn so much money that you have to pay a six-figure tax bill?*

So I asked him.

He told me he started his career as a radio DJ but noticed the people driving the nice cars into the studio all worked in sales and marketing. So, he pivoted into those departments and worked his way up to a high level of a prominent media company, earned a seven-figure bonus, and thus now had a six-figure tax bill.

For me, this was a light bulb moment.

I had no idea that people in business could make so much money. I thought only rock stars, movie stars, and pro athletes had that capability.

At this point in my career, I knew I was good at what I did, but I was tapped out in terms of time and earning potential.

I remembered Tony's advice, and I began modeling this client's path. I started studying sales and marketing like crazy. I started reading lots of books, watching webinars, and attending live workshops.

As I learned better sales and marketing strategies, my business took off. I was able to leave the world of working for someone else and grow my first multiple-six-figure training business.

I grew my first business and leveraged time because I used an old business law that said something like this: It's easier to deliver more products to an existing customer than it is to go and find new customers. So, I asked my clients what else they wanted to help them feel healthier and give them more energy.

After listening to what they told me and continuing to pursue my education on how to help people live their healthiest and most vibrant lives, I added functional medicine protocols, supplements, in-home cooking services, massage, custom diet plans, and on and on.

This pushed me to get certified as a functional medicine practitioner and a metabolic typing advisor, pursue yoga and qigong certifications, and more. My idea at this moment in time was to be everything my clients needed.

When I returned from a live seminar, I would naturally talk about what I had learned while away. One day, one of my clients invited me to teach his marketing department the strategies I'd learned.

At the end of my hour-long presentation, he handed me a check for $5,000! I thought, *Holy crap, that was a lot of fun, and it pays much better than my work as a trainer!* This unlocked a whole new area of my business I had never imagined before.

As I told other clients about my presentation, many of them seemed interested in having me speak to their employees. Several of them said, "If you did it for them, would you do it for our business, too?"

This is what launched me from a six-figure to a seven-figure mindset.

After helping others achieve massive growth in their businesses and growing my own to earn millions of dollars, I started to realize that helping big businesses was not MY actual story and not the best way I could use my knowledge and experience to serve others.

Even though I was having fun and working with several wealthy and ultra-wealthy clients helping them in various ways to grow their businesses, I could feel that something inside me was not right.

It was 2017, and I invested even more time and money into my personal development. I decided to attend the Tony Robbins "Unleash the Power Within" event to give myself the space to acknowledge and explore what I had been feeling.

As you know, my own story started with having nothing, and I've seen exactly how it's possible to become a multimillionaire.

At Unleash the Power Within, it came to me that my passion lies with serving entrepreneurs that are making six figures and want to grow to seven figures and beyond while becoming financially independent and happy. I could feel it deep down in my heart. I got the clarity I was after, and I made the shift.

Using Tony's concept of modeling, I sat down and asked myself, *With all the information at people's fingertips today, why don't more entrepreneurs find their next level of success?*

With this question in mind, I left for an entire week to stay at a retreat that inspires me (one I have a vision of owning one day!) It is a gorgeous property in an area with hiking trails, waterfalls, and lots of wildlife. There is a library filled with every type of book imaginable, massage services, and delectable food. I was filled with inspiration and was ready to dig in and figure this out.

The main question I was asking myself is this: "What separates people who accomplish their hopes and dreams from those who don't?"

When I got the answer, it hit me like a ton of bricks.

The key to success is at the foundational level of how we live our lives.

It came to me that every successful (wealthy and ultra-wealthy) client I worked with had high levels of personal development. They also exercised, ate nutritious foods, managed a healthy weight, went to bed and woke up at the same times daily, wrote in a journal or planner, set goals, and built in accountability.

I just kept saying, "Be. Do. Have."

I didn't make up that phrase. I wish I had, but these three words would become the foundation of success for all entrepreneurs trying to reach their next level.

If you're not familiar with the idea of "Be, Do, Have," let me give you a quick explanation. It simply says you need to "Be" the person you want to be to "Do" the things you need to do, and that will equal "Having" what you want to have.

Most people get this backward and will say something like this: If I just "Had" the money then I would "Do" the things I need to do so I could finally "Be" happy. This kind of thinking is backward, and it never creates lasting success.

When I combined this concept of "Be, Do, Have" with the concept of modeling, my entire framework for coaching entrepreneurs permanently shifted, and the results for clients started skyrocketing. It became instantly clear that when they got stuck in their business, we could look at "who" they were currently "being" and create a path for change.

Information about how to do anything is easier to find than ever. Entrepreneurs don't lack information, but they likely aren't getting the *correct* information for where they currently are in their business.

There are two problems with this:

1. Today's entrepreneur doesn't realize that THEY are the bottleneck in the growth of their business.

2. They typically keep asking *how* to do something instead of *who* can do the thing that needs to be done.

Today, entrepreneurs need the correct information at the right time, not all the information all the time. That's completely overwhelming and doesn't work.

The overall process toward guaranteed success is straightforward yet powerful.

Step 1: Get clear on where you currently are, both personally and professionally.

This step is more critical than anything else you will ever do. Getting clear on where you are is the beginning of having a chance to get where you want to go.

Imagine trying to get to Disney World, but you have no idea where you are starting from. This is the same idea in your personal and business life. If you don't know where you are, you have very little chance of getting where you want to go.

Step 2: Get clear on where you are going.

Knowing where you are and where you are going is the rocket fuel that will propel you forward to DO what's required for you to get there.

Step 3: Get a clear plan on how to go from where you are to where you are going.

When you become the person who knows where you are, where you want to go, and how to get there, then you can HAVE the dream life you've imagined.

That's it.

Of course, the first step in finding out where you are is discovering *who you are BE-ing*. My favorite tool for uncovering this aspect of yourself—that clients have told me is a game changer—is called the "Perfect Average Week."

The Perfect Average Week tool is designed to give you full permission and freedom to design your weeks precisely the way you want to so that you feel amazing as you move your business and life forward. Here's the link for you to try this tool out for free: JayAltman.com/PerfectAverageWeek

And if you'd like the training I use to help entrepreneurs understand the three EXACT steps they need to take to go from where they are to where they want to be in their business and finances, you can gain access here:

JayAltman.com/Application

CHAPTER FOURTEEN

CHRIS CLEAR

Chris Clear

Chris Clear is the founder and president of Clear Storage Group, LLC, as well as the founder of The Clear Group, LLC, and Rock Springs Self Storage, LLC. He also serves as president of Accurate Payment Solutions and sales manager for Atlantic Merchant Services of East Tennessee and Southwest Virginia.

He lives with his rock star wife and three daughters in the great state of Tennessee. His background includes a successful career in business-to-business corporate sales before becoming a business owner himself. Chris owns several businesses, ranging from e-commerce to self-storage facilities. His successful track record has led him to coach and consult business owners, especially those in the self-storage industry.

When he's not working, you can find him spending time with his family or doing almost anything outdoors.

SELF-STORAGE
SECRETS

As I stood there with my phone in my hand, reality hit hard. Confusion washed over me, and I couldn't believe that something like this could be happening. After all, I had followed the pathway to success, step-by-step ...

"Hello, Chris. I need you to stop what you're doing and bring your laptop to the office," my manager said.

"Why, what's going on? You do remember my wife and I had a baby six days ago ... right?" I replied.

"Chris. I'm not asking you to come to the office and bring your laptop. I'm telling you!" he snapped back.

"OK, but I don't understand why I need to come to the office ... What's so urgent? I mean, it's not like I'm getting fired or something ... is it?" I asked.

"Chris, bring your laptop to the office and be here at 2 p.m."... Click.

I had been a top-producing sales rep in my office every year, and I was also a top sales rep in my region and the company. How in the world could someone who produced so much be in a position where they are being let go? None of it made sense.

What could've happened to cause this?

At that moment, I realized things were going to change—no, things *had* to change! One phone call and meeting completely changed the trajectory of my world.

I went from being the breadwinner of my household to jobless with no idea what to do. I never dreamed that something like this could happen to me. Not only was I jobless, but I had a wife and three daughters counting on me to be there for them.

Talk about pressure.

To make matters worse, I was being let go in the middle of one of the worst economies the US had seen in decades. I found myself applying for jobs with hundreds of other candidates.

Many of these companies required the same 60- to 80-hour workweek, but the pay was less than half of what I made before. The choices in front of me were bleak.

I was also in a place where I had other challenges to overcome to find a new job. One of the biggest ones resulted from a decision I had made years ago. You see, I spent too much time having fun and not enough time making the grades to finish college. I didn't have a degree.

And every one of those jobs required a degree.

I've always felt that you could thrive in sales without a degree. To my credit, I'd been able to excel at doing that very thing … Well, at least until that point. Yet, I found myself trying to decide if I should go back to school to get a degree. My other option was to accept a position that would pay approximately one-third of my previous income.

Even with lower pay, those jobs still had all the same requirements of travel and time.

To say it was one of the darkest times in my life would be putting it mildly. My pity party didn't last long before I started to rethink the possibilities.

Within a few weeks, I was able to network with friends and find a new position. Although I would be making less money than I'd made in the past, there was potential to make more down the road.

I was grateful to have found a position, but I couldn't shake the feeling that the same thing could happen again. That fear was very real for both myself and my wife. What would we do if this happened again? How much longer would we have to delay our lifestyle? How were we going to make up for the lost savings?

With all these questions filling my mind, I realized the only way to overcome the issues with those jobs I'd applied for would be to go into business for myself. A business of my own. It would be risky, but the freedom I could achieve for myself and my family must be worth the risk.

You see, we've all been there at some point in our lives. Things don't go the way we want them to and we must decide what's next. People complain about losing their job but will return to working for someone else. When they do this, chances are the same thing will happen to them again.

Experts say almost everyone thinks about being their own boss. And yet, only a small percentage of people do it. I had plenty of prior job experiences to help me with this new business. I had a successful background in sales, which is essential in any industry. I also had experience in marketing and advertising.

In 2011, when this took place, I wasn't sure where I'd be today. As of 2021, I own several businesses, including quite a few self-storage facilities. To say it's been a journey would be an understatement!

For the first year—or even the first few years—*I was paralyzed with fear.*

It wasn't your normal fear … It was a debilitating fear that I would make the wrong decision. And it wasn't just one decision that caused the anxiety; it was almost every decision.

The problem with that fear was that I was taking NO action … None. Zip. Zilch. Nada. I spent my time analyzing what could go wrong instead of looking at what could go right. Like I said, *paralyzed.*

Then, one day it hit me. The companies I'd worked for in the past had no problem entrusting me with millions of dollars of their revenue. *If they were willing to put that much trust into me, why wouldn't I do the same thing?*

I realized that imperfect action beats perfect inaction every single time.

There will never be a perfect time or product or service; there is *only now.* I already knew how to sell, and to be successful in business, you must have sales to drive income.

You must also have an effective marketing and advertising campaign. The marketing will help generate interest in the products or services you sell. And that interest is what leads to increased sales.

I had the background; now I needed to use it!

I'd been through the good times and the bad, so I could relate to those who had "the plan" and then got punched in the mouth! So I learned to put my skills to work, trust my instincts, and make the calls when needed.

When I worked for other companies, I went all in. Now it was time to do the same for me.

I'd broken sales records in previous jobs. I'd even broken income records in my office. It seemed silly to think that I could do those things for someone else's company and not do the same for mine.

The recognition of my skills combined with the determination to make something happen helped me see a way to *make* things happen. I began to bring on new clients to each of my businesses. I also began to get recognition within my community as the "Go-to-Guy" for anyone needing help with their business.

Having been in a position where all my income was taken away so quickly, I became driven to make sure that wouldn't happen again. I hadn't taken the advice I'd heard my grandmother give me so many times throughout my childhood. Whenever I'd choose one big gift over several smaller ones, she'd always say, "Don't put all your eggs in one basket."

When she said it the first time, I didn't understand what she meant. I asked her, and she explained, "If you only get one gift, it might be bigger or shinier than several smaller gifts. The problem," she said, "is what happens if you don't like that one gift? What if you lose it? What if it breaks? Now, your one gift is gone. If you have several gifts, though, if you don't like one, or one gets lost or breaks, you still have others to enjoy."

You see, I'd put all my eggs in one basket when I worked for someone else with no other way to create an income for myself. I'd started to take my grandmother's advice … but I still needed something that could do *more* for myself and my family.

There are lots of ways to invest in real estate. Some people become real estate investors by purchasing a rental house or two. Others may buy a duplex or a small apartment complex. Still, others may choose to invest money with a REIT (Real Estate Investment Trust) or a Syndication.

All of those are viable options for successful real estate investments.

When I looked at each of those, there were things that I liked but others that I didn't care for.

For example, if I purchased a rental home, a duplex, or even a small apartment complex, I'd be responsible for everything from collecting the rent to handling repairs from unruly renters. Since I would be starting small, I wouldn't have the additional cash flow to pay someone to do the repairs, which would mean I would need to do them. If you have a background in the trades, that might be an option for you. It would be riskier for me to try the repairs than to pay someone who knows what they're doing!

My venture into the real estate world came through purchasing a self-storage facility. I had several important reasons for going this route.

1. You have many renters that pay you each month, not just one.

2. If someone doesn't pay, you can have them moved out of their unit within one month. This will limit lost revenue.

3. There is no plumbing or electrical maintenance to perform on storage units.

4. Rates on self-storage units increase year after year.

5. You can automate nearly the entire process of renting a self-storage unit, which reduces the need for employees.

After buying the first facility, I looked at the processes the previous owner had and focused on ways to use them and improve them. Some of the processes were good, while others made me want to pull my hair out!

One of the first things I did was to look at the cash flow and see how the payments were coming in. Many of the renters paid each month by having a credit or debit card on file, which automatically gets charged on the first of each month. Those are the renters we never have issues with getting their payments.

Other renters, however, would mail a check whenever it was convenient for them. And an entirely different group of renters would offer to pay in cash, but only if I would drive to their home or work to collect the rent.

With a goal to own quite a few facilities, there was no way I wanted to drive all over town picking up checks or cash. We had to automate the payment process for everyone if we were ever going to scale.

By making it mandatory to pay by a credit or debit card each month automatically, we were able to control when we're paid and go from renters paying three weeks late or more to each unit being paid by the 5th of the month. That one change improved cash flow and reduced the stress I was dealing with more than anything else we'd done.

Our next project was to correct the unit pricing. The previous owners of that facility had a habit of inconsistent pricing. If someone asked for a small 5x10 unit that rented for $35 per month and none were available, they rented them a larger unit for the same $35 per month.

They did this even when the larger unit customarily rented for $95 per month. By doing this, the previous owners severely limited their income ... and ours too!

We adjusted the pricing on each unit as renters left, and soon, most of the units were rented at the correct rate. This step helped increase our cash flow without adding additional units.

Next, we tackled the process of renting a unit. I sought ways to allow anyone looking for a unit to see the availability and pricing through our website. Automation is vital if you plan to own a single facility or several. It's even more critical if you plan to hold them as investments while maintaining a job working for someone else.

These are just some of the first steps I use when acquiring a new facility. The best part is that we find new ways to improve the process and new challenges to overcome with each new purchase.

I've become passionate about this industry because I love helping people.

When I speak with our renters, it's evident that many of them are going through a difficult time in their lives. Some may be going through a new marriage, while others may be going through a divorce. Others may need storage due to a birth, while others deal with losing a loved one.

I take the trust our renters place in us very seriously because they're storing things in our care that are important to them.

Doing your due diligence when looking at any new investment, whether a self-storage facility or any other piece of property, is crucial. Keep in mind the things mentioned above when you're doing your homework. If you can skip any of those steps because the seller already has them in place, you'll be miles ahead!

My goal is to be as helpful as possible. So, if you've been through something as traumatic as losing a job without a backup plan or if you've found yourself in a place where you never thought you'd be, I would like you to think about these questions and answer them honestly:

- If you lost your job once or more, due to no fault of your own, do you think that it could happen again?

- If it does happen again, are you willing to take steps to have a financial safety net in place?

After all, most of you will have to deal with job cuts, downsizing, or similar scenarios. How great would it be to know that if something like that happened to you, your family would be fine? Can you imagine the feeling of knowing that you've done what it takes to create a secondary or side income?

Imagine what it would be like to start a business that you and your family can run for years. Now, imagine being able to turn that business over to your children to run. That single purchase can be the driver that changes your family's financial future for generations.

When you increase your income, you can potentially invest it, pay off debt, pay for your children's college, buy a new car, retire early, or buy a new house. Your dream may not be a new car, vacations, or extra spending money. Your dream may be security for you and your family.

Self-storage isn't for everyone, but those who become part of our storage family learn and share all there is to know about storage, both the good and the bad. Our team looks out for each other because when you make more money through something like self-storage, you're also helping countless other families in their time of need.

Since each person's scenario is different, our team will get to know you and discover exactly what you want out of the self-storage industry. Be prepared for a great chat about where you are now and where you want to go.

My goal isn't to sell you a package but to see what options are the best fit *for you*. My team will provide you with the resources it takes to make an informed decision, whether you're looking to buy a self-storage facility, build one, or invest in one as a silent partner.

If you're interested in learning more about how to increase your income through self-storage, visit:

ChrisClear.net

CHAPTER FIFTEEN

BARRY GABSTER

Barry Gabster

Barry Gabster is the Founder and CEO of InitiateU, Inc., an integrated direct response marketing agency. He is an expert in marketing strategy for B2C professional, financial, business, and home services industries. Barry makes time to mentor young professionals, support Big Brothers/Big Sisters, and volunteer for the Orange County Pit Bull Rescue.

NICE DOESN'T ALWAYS
FINISH LAST

I didn't start out with a Million Dollar Identity. I started out as the short kid who got bullied all the time. In middle school, I was about as tall as the average nine-year-old boy—a whopping 4'2"—by far, the shortest boy in my school.

Fortunately, I lived near L.A., and I was television commercial material. My parents had so much confidence in me that they got me into acting at a young age. I had some success with roles in Chick-Fil-A commercials and a spot for K-Mart during the 1988 Olympics, but I hated it.

Even though running to auditions kept me from being picked on by other kids, it also meant that half my days were spent in the car with my mom. I couldn't participate in afterschool activities. I could never meet up with friends. I had no life of my own. I was miserable.

I ended up pitching fits and begged my parents to let me go back to having a normal life. When they finally relented, I started spending more time with kids my age. But that meant more chances for bullying. Talk about being between a rock and a hard place.

But I was always a problem solver, so my wheels were turning. *How can I combat being the short kid who gets bullied all the time?*

My first thought was to surround myself with more people. I would just make friends with everybody. I became a social butterfly, and it made all the difference.

That one choice changed everything for the rest of my life.

That was my way of overcoming my height issues, overcoming my lack of self-confidence. I had so many friends that nobody could pick on me because if I ever got into any type of fight or tussle, I had enough backup to make sure that I was always the winner in the fight.

I've got plenty of friends that will tell you I, unfortunately, got into a lot of fights and maybe antagonized fights. But we always won the fights with the exception of one, *the big one*, which I started.

It was about 12:30 p.m. and I was squeezing into the car with my friends. Our car was parked very tightly between two other cars, and it just so happened to be right in front of a skinhead party.

We were stuck, so stuck we couldn't leave. We had to engage with the skinheads and ended up antagonizing a fight and getting pulled out of the car that I was in, laid out on the grass. One of the skinheads got on top of me and another one took his steel toe boot and kicked me in the head multiple times, literally smashing my face, leaving me with a broken eye socket and a broken nose.

I will never forget laying in a gurney bed and having a doctor standing over me, pushing my nose across my face while listening to crushing bones get moved back in place. It was so loud ... I heard it inside my brain. It was the loudest noise I had ever heard. It was brutal.

That fight was my biggest loss, but my friends and I actually won it even though my face got wrecked. At that point, I kind of became somebody. I became somebody *in my own mind* because I had this team. I had this group of people. That's what it really comes down to is the group, right?

It moved on to becoming my brotherhood. And from there, I moved to hosting house parties when my parents would allow me. There were hundreds and hundreds of people coming to my parties.

Then it turned into annual Christmas parties, and I'd have some of the best DJs in the world come to my house party or my holiday party. I'd pay them money and I wouldn't charge any entrance fees. All I wanted was for my friends and other people to show up and say that Barry threw this ridiculous party.

And it was all done in an attempt to gain more friends.

I eventually got through high school, but unlike most of my friends, I didn't have money for some prestigious school. And I sure didn't have the grades I needed to get into college. I was a social butterfly. I was the one who was trying to make friends and go out to all the parties and befriend people.

After watching my father grow up working for Bimbo Bakeries as a delivery man, throwing bread off a truck for pretty much his entire career, and watching him struggle through that just to make ends meet so he could provide us with the life that we both hoped for, I knew I wasn't college material.

My father was always chasing the next best thing. He had plenty of side hustles, but they all came in the form of multi-level marketing, and quite frankly, this wasn't something that I was interested in. It was at this point that I made a commitment to myself. That's *not what I'm going to do. I'm not following in my dad's footsteps. I'm going to be in corporate America.*

For me, the big prize would be to go to work every day wearing a suit. Well dressed and carrying a briefcase, I could envision myself in a desk job, not doing back-breaking work as a laborer. That's when I decided to pursue my dream of working in corporate America.

I made the decision to enroll in three different temp agencies. I set out to become somebody that my father wasn't and somebody that I knew I wanted to be … But I wasn't sure who that person was.

After a few years of trying to figure out what I wanted to do, trying to climb the corporate ladder, I ended up back in sales, which is right back to where I've always been.

I had started my career as a short, stuck at 4'2" child actor, with a lack of self-confidence but still able to land a few commercials. And then suddenly, I'm selling people on *me* and selling them products and services for money—money I didn't see when I was doing commercials as a kid.

It was then I determined what I was destined to do. I was destined to talk to people. I was destined to commiserate with people. And I was destined to identify with people and all the problems they have because, at the end of the day, we all have them, right? And if I can make money doing it in the interim, then it's just a win-win all around.

When I found out sales was my thing, I pushed forward on it. After a few years of working as a partner with a marketing agency, I eventually started my own advertising agency.

But I don't actually advertise my agency, which is the most ironic thing in the world. Because I've made a career out of making friends, my agency has grown to well over seven figures annually through word of mouth.

I built a career out of making friends. I often receive compliments about my ability to adapt and find relevance with some of the oddest of characters. At this stage of my life, it's not even a thought for me.

In your career, it's important you get your customer to become your friend. This is how you retain your customers forever and how you build a solid customer base and a thriving business.

The best clients are the ones who will work with you through tough times. Those are my clients. Those are my friends. But building a successful business requires more than just making friends. It also requires a strong work ethic.

My grandfather taught me the meaning of a good work ethic. I grew up building his ranch at the age of six, putting stakes in the ground, and building the fence around his five-acre ranch in the rain. I did what no kid would do at that age, and to this day, he still tells that story for anybody who will listen.

Work ethic has been ingrained in my bones. It was so much so that I worked two jobs to pay for the perfect wedding for my wife and me, even though I only got four hours of sleep a night for over a year.

Sure, I had a strong work ethic, but I was a dreamer, so I would fall short. I often disappointed my wife talking about career ideas and more often than not, they wouldn't come to fruition. She finally said something that I live my life by every day, "Prior Planning Prevents Piss Poor Performance."

The 6 P's. So simple.

I now apply the 6 P's to my everyday life, and it has become the basis for everything I do because actions speak louder than words. If you say you are going to do something, then you need to do it.

When I meet prospective clients, I know that I can deliver results based on my work history and work ethic. I just need to get them to know, like, and trust me. What I'm about to share with you flows so naturally for me now that I don't even think about it. It's a technique you will need to work on.

First, I wake up and I know I am going to be "selling." I put that in quotes because I hate the term "selling." I prefer to think of myself as an educator or a conversationalist. I always start thinking of the first three questions that I'm going to use to get past the defensive wall that everybody has up before letting it down and ultimately letting you in.

The first impression is the last thing they will ever remember. This goes beyond how you look and how you are dressed, this applies specifically to phone sales. And nobody can see how you are dressed over the phone.

The approach, whether in-person or over the phone, needs to be thought out.

Think about this. What is your opening question?

Think about something that will make them say more than one word. An open-ended question that ignites them to give you more information.

I don't use the normal "How are you doing?" This often results in a one-word answer such as "good," "great," or "okay." Another great example is the standard, "How is the weather today?" Both examples give a one-word answer.

Instead, I'm going with, "Can you believe this weather lately?" And if in person, I'm literally shaking my head for the effect it will give. Or if I'm on the phone, I'm giving a slight giggle, ensuring that I'm smiling through it because the customer can feel your smile.

And if you get them to smile, you are officially in.

My question is involved. It asks them about the weather today and discusses how the weather has been by adding the word *lately*. It would be very hard for an individual to answer this question in one word.

I know this seems elementary and generic but, in most circumstances, I will get at least a five-word answer to this question. A five-word answer is the equivalent of about two seconds which gives me enough time to think of the second question that will be more about them.

The idea here is to get your customer talking. As they're talking, you need to be consistently curating your next question. While you're thinking about your second and third questions, it's crucial that you actively listen. Engage with eye contact.

It's no secret that people like to talk about themselves. So, ask yourself what chord you can strike in your questioning that will make them comfortable enough to drop their guard and allow you in.

Of course, the first question has always been the easiest. While they are answering my first question, I prep my second and third questions. Open-ended questions that give you five or more seconds make this process much easier. From there, it's easy to build a relationship. I've built my entire career around building relationships.

Now, I do what I want to do on my schedule.

I make all the money I want to make. There's no hitting an income ceiling. And now I am my own boss. I can sit on the beach with my laptop and work all day, which of course, I think is everybody's end game, being able to work wherever you want, being able to travel as much as you want, work wherever in the world you want, and make as much as you want.

But the way that you get there is by building relationships.

If you're looking for a marketing agency that will build a long-term relationship with you—an agency that will treat you like a friend instead of just another customer, then reach out to us for a free 30-minute strategy call.

InitiateU.life

CHAPTER SIXTEEN

ROBERT NICKELL

Robert Nickell

Robert Nickell is an accomplished real estate investor and entrepreneur in the business process outsourcing (BPO) industry. He is CEO of Dallas-based Rocket Station, which he founded in 2018. Rocket Station recruits and trains college-educated Filipino professionals to fulfill a variety of remote roles at small to midsize American companies. Under Nickell's leadership, Rocket Station has become a multimillion dollar company with 10% month-over-month growth since early 2020. Rocket Station is the second BPO company Nickell has founded. For four years, he co-owned Dallas-based Investor Virtual Assistant Services, which provided outsourcing services specifically to the real estate vertical. Previously, he owned the Dallas realty investment firm, GreenRo Homes. Nickell earned his BA in business and communications from Austin College in 2009.

FROM IMPOSTER
TO EMPIRE-BUILDER

'll never forget the day my then-wife wanted to go Christmas shopping at Nordstrom. She believed the image I had created—that I was a young, rolling-in-money, real estate success story. Yet I was on the verge of a panic attack because I didn't know if my credit card would go through.

She picked up a white T-shirt. I looked down at the price tag: $80. I knew I was in trouble.

My friends, my family, my mastermind groups, everyone thought I was a brilliant success. But it was all a charade. At that moment, I experienced absolute clarity about the nightmare I had trapped myself in and knew something had to change. I just didn't know where to turn.

After college, I worked in a traditional management role for two years at a company I didn't care about, a medical debt purchaser. After two years of hating that job, I jumped into real estate.

I left my job for freedom, but I created my own prison. Eighteen months later, I began experiencing anxiety attacks. I had started attending real estate masterminds and comparing myself to the guys claiming big revenue amounts. I was spending more than I was making because I thought I needed to reinvest in my business and myself.

But I knew nothing about margins or systems or processes. I was a one-man show en route to rapid burnout. I was in complete overwhelm trying to keep up appearances, while in reality missing calls, missing deadlines, and missing out on my life! I worked 80+ hours per week, and my business was in complete chaos. My pride and ego were on the line.

One day, a tornado went through Wiley, Texas. My broker, Wes, bought lumber, loaded it on a trailer, and donated supplies and his time to help rebuild.

How was that possible for him?

I suddenly realized that Wes had what I wanted: a happy marriage, time and money to help neighbors in need and to take family vacations, energy to build go-karts in the garage with his son, and a schedule that let him attend his daughter's golf tournaments even if they were mid-week. His lifestyle wasn't ostentatious and yet he had everything. So I went to see him.

Full of emotion, I spilled all my overwhelm and fear out to Wes. He interrupted me, asking if I wanted to keep complaining or if I wanted a solution. That was my big "aha!" moment. He showed me that I was my problem. He looked at me and said, "Brother, you got the same number of hours in the day as Beyoncé." I needed that laugh!

He told me that his *team* did the day-to-day work of business. They followed the scripts, systems, and processes he'd created. I complained that I had tried to hire people but couldn't find anyone good. He challenged me, yet again: Did I think people intentionally got up in the morning to do a bad job at work? The realization hit me hard. Of course not!

Like so many other entrepreneurs, I'd trapped myself into thinking nobody could do my work better than me. I had no systems in place, and I didn't know how to interview, onboard, or train someone effectively. Because I wouldn't give up control, I'd lost control completely.

And then Wes changed my life and its trajectory. He shared his SOPs, scripts, scope of work, and the foundation he built his business upon. That meeting with Wes was a turning point for me. I learned to accept responsibility for my business's shortcomings. My current success is thanks in part to Wes sharing his successful business framework with me.

I quickly realized that being an expert in residential real estate was not enough. A business requires a foundational structure in place to allow the owner to have a life outside of work.

Because I'd had a breakdown and then a breakthrough, I started sharing what I'd learned. Free of charge. I worked with 73 people, one on one, asking what they wanted to accomplish. We started with the end goal in mind. I gave them the resources to create systems and processes for their business, so they could hire and train staff.

Can you guess what happened?

They didn't want to do it. Instead, I had people asking me every day, "Will you just do this for me?" I thought that giving someone the tools they need is all that was necessary to be successful. But I learned that not everyone has the desire, willpower, or energy to implement processes themselves. And business owners shouldn't have to be experts in recruiting, interviewing, and training.

So I decided to train people. I woke up at 4 a.m. every day. I practiced real estate until 1 p.m. then took a break. From 2 p.m. to 8 p.m., I was training. From 8 p.m. until midnight, I met virtually with my team to organize the next day. I was back at it again at 4 the next morning. I did that for over two years!

During the 2 p.m. to 8 p.m. period, I held Skype calls and hosted daily in-person staff training for small groups. The other part of the training was individual calls with each of the 73 people—my "clients." I interviewed them regarding their goals, I worked with them to build out their business plan, I created scopes of work and scripts. I built a foundation to recruit and train the right people so that I could pair skill sets with the needs of the client.

I used my real estate business as the training ground. Once the staff trainees finished their two-week training period, they got work experience in my business. By the time a client interviewed a trainee, they already knew how to do what the client needed. If you're thinking this doesn't sound sustainable, you are correct!

After a few years, I had to choose between real estate and the staffing business I'd created. The staffing business filled a gap in the market, for myself and for others, but I did all the work for free. The real estate business supported everything, so neither was profitable. I was also going through a messy divorce at the time. Probably not surprising since, even though I was physically present, I was not present in any other way in my marriage because I worked so much. I was young, overworked, and exhausted.

It hit me one day in my attorney's office that I had no real direction. I had always thought real estate would be my livelihood and let me retire comfortably. I decided to give the business to my soon-to-be ex-wife, and it was a huge emotional release for me. That was in 2015. By the end of 2021—even during a global pandemic—my company, Rocket Station, has over 1,400 employees and 500 clients.

For the first time in my life, I don't have any imposter syndrome. I don't feel like a fraud in any way. I don't have to lie about my numbers. I don't have to brag about top-line revenue because I've *achieved* it, with no money on the other side. I understand what it means to operate a business that serves other people in their needs. That's what Rocket Station does for clients—and can do for you.

I offer a service that enhances the lives of my clients, their businesses, and the lives of my employees in a sustainable way. I had 98.4% attendance last year from my VAs. Do you know how many millions of work hours that represents? And that's happening while I spend a month in the jungle in Mexico on a spiritual journey, meeting with shamans. My life has completely changed from the days when I slept less than four hours each night.

Our sweet spot is helping companies that have 10–200 employees, and we make up about 15% of their total workforce. However, our average client hires just one to two people. I listened to a discovery call—the introductory phase conducted by our sales team—recently. The potential client, Allison Weiss, told us that she "eats, breathes, and sleeps work." I've been there, and I know how overwhelming it is to live in that state.

As our team inquired about her goals and her business, she finally said, "I can't work 14-hour days. This is not the business that I want. I'm not able to serve people the way I need to because I'm stretched thin. I don't do anything really well because I've got too much to do." How many of us can relate to that?

After a discovery call, a prospect can commit to a Process Mapping call, where we map out their business processes. On this call, the business owners realize our expertise. They are not just hiring a VA or outsourcing something insignificant; they are teaming up with us as partners. On that call, Allison's energy shifted when she realized together we would create the business of her dreams.

At first, clients assume we're going to provide a VA who is uneducated and unable to communicate, from a third world country, with language and cultural barriers. Every person who reaches out to us has started a day with a 400-item task list, 398 of which are still there at the end of the day, with new ones to be added tomorrow. When they interview with our staff, they meet individuals who are sharp, professional, educated, with impressive resumes and clean background checks. Our clients are delighted with the quality of our staff every time and have a hard time choosing just one candidate.

When our clients have tried hiring in-house, they quickly become frustrated with the results, and their customers experience subpar service. Invariably, the managers and the business owners step in, and they can't focus on their work because they're putting out fires. Fires are to business as diseases are to the body—a message that something is wrong and changes need to be made. But you must use a new approach if you want different results. That's where we come in.

Working with us is a game-changer for our clients. We service a wide range of industries because many of the core functions are the same for every business. Every client comes to us with a very specific pain point. They think they need specific skill sets. We know they need people with motivation, drive, a growth mindset, accountability, desire to excel, and the ability to communicate. They can be taught a specific skill quickly as long as they possess these characteristics.

Once we find the right person, we train them with you to get them up to speed. We provide staff for customized support, inside sales, social media, and general administrative tasks. You tell us about your fires, and we implement systems and processes to deliver calm, profitable, consistent, and predictable operations.

It isn't just about business. It's about how business affects your life! Customer service managers feel it's impossible to meet their boss's expectations and quotas. Husbands are stressed because they missed the kids' soccer games *again*. Moms feel guilty because they aren't spending enough time with their teenage daughters. People want balance in their lives. Allison recently completed our process and called to thank me for exactly that.

She said, "Hiring Jaja gave me the life of my dreams. I am able to be the person and live the life that I'm supposed to because of what you've created." Allison is now a digital nomad, running a successful business in commercial real estate. She hosts her own podcast. She told me working with Rocket Station gave her stability, consistency, appreciation, gratitude, and profit. Allison finally relaxed and trusted the process. And it not only changed her life, but it also changed her team's lives as well.

My purpose with Rocket Station is to help my clients and my staff achieve everything that they desire. At the end of the day, nobody just wants money. They want to be better parents, spouses, and friends. They want to build relationships and connections and have time for creativity and fun. That's what people care about.

A client in Memphis explained, "We signed up with you guys because we're saving over $3.5 million in salary expense. We're staying with you guys because of the emotional capital we get. Our teams are highly functioning. As an organization, we're more efficient. There's less chaos. Less emotional baggage. We came for the money. We're staying because we got our lives back."

Working with us is a three-phase process. The first phase is the discovery call. I don't participate in that decision-making process because I trust my team and the systems we have in place, They are experts in business, staffing, and workforce management. The goal is for the client to assess if they want to work with us, and for us to evaluate if they are a good fit.

Once we have agreed we are a fit, the client moves to the process mapping phase. We learn in-depth about the structure, processes, systems, goals, tasks, routines, and metrics of the client's business. We then create the systems and processes needed to run your business in a replicable, predictable way. We map out this process, including detailed job descriptions, over a few Zoom calls. We are sensitive to the fact that people can get defensive and protective at this stage. Clients are justifiably frustrated, and we simply ask that they trust us to get them the outcomes they desire—because we can, and we do!

Next, we help you interview, onboard, and train the right person for the job, with the goal of creating stability and minimizing turnover. You want staff in roles that are fulfilling, that motivate them to accomplish the necessary tasks. Lastly, we continue to work behind the scenes, making sure our employees and you have what you need to be successful. Our clients often share the emotional relief and extreme confidence they feel after going through our process. They can now achieve their goals *and* enjoy life!

Here's another example of a company that profited by transitioning from chaos to focus. When Dave and RJ first came to us, they wanted to hire someone to help them scale multiple lines of business. Their primary audience is professionals—doctors, lawyers, consultants—who want to safely invest in real estate without expending much time or effort. They wanted to build out their team to add verticals such as property management and investment.

I pushed back. I asked them to focus on the area that produces the most revenue for them. I then told them a story. My dad was our high school basketball coach, and he always said that as long as the team is winning, everyone is happy. When you stop winning, issues pop up everywhere. It's the same in business. As long as you have money, problems can be addressed without too much stress.

Our first goal with all our clients is to achieve the stability of consistent revenue; that's the lifeblood of your business. Dave and RJ decided on hiring someone to help with sales. Three years ago they hired Bell, and today, their business is flourishing. They no longer suffer from being spread too thin. They have quadrupled their prior revenue and eliminated unnecessary overhead.

Rocket Station is a leading business process outsourcing provider for innovative companies. We eliminate the difficulties of in-house hiring by providing you with one or more dedicated team members. We hire and train top-notch VAs to help you build an efficient, scalable, and profitable business that delivers a world-class customer experience. First, we pay our team members well and provide other benefits, such as healthcare, so the team is stable and has consistency. Second, to be clear, our clients are not hiring employees from Rocket Station. RS provides our clients with dedicated VA services for a flat fee. The result is no liability for our clients.

At our core, we bring stability to your life and business. We tailor our approach to your unique needs. Each of our team members has over two years of experience in Business Process Outsourcing, Virtual Staffing, Customer Service, Business to Business Solutions, Project Management, Small Business Support, Lead Generation, and more.

Working with Rocket Station is about getting the support you need from a team of experts who can deliver outstanding results. You don't have to feel alone and lost and overwhelmed as you grow your business. You don't have to give up your personal life to be successful. If you are ready to take the leap to a happier, healthier business and existence, book a call with us today!

RocketStation.com/call-booking-page

CHAPTER SEVENTEEN

LORI LYNN

Lori Lynn

Lori Lynn is the senior editor of *Million Dollar Identity* and the founder of a ghostwriting and book-editing business for self-published authors called DragonflyWings.Ink. Host of the *Rise and Climb* podcast, CEO of Happily Unemployable LLC, and co-author of the book *Unemployable: Confessions of a Serial Killer's Kid* with Timothy R. Johnson, she lives in Nashville, TN.

Before she became a single mom of three remarkable children, she traveled the U.S. as a spokesperson, motivational speaker, and commercial actor while pursuing a bachelor's degree in corporate communications and writing.

She has been described as a "book ninja" by Dan Henry, a "genius book architect" by Myron Golden, "so much more than a book editor" by David Keesee, "the queen of editing" by Michelle Cunningham, and "the best editor I have had the pleasure of working with and the true definition of a superhuman" by Kiana Danial. Her superpower is making influencers look as smart on the page as they sound from the stage.

JUST SAY "YES"
AND KEEP SAYING "YES"

"Get in the van! We've got to go!"

My girls and I made our way down our long, gravel driveway, but just before we got to the end, we noticed a sign:

FOR SALE

"Mom! What's that?"

"Why's that there?"

"Is that for us?"

"Mom!"

My heart was racing. I had visited my landlady in the hospital over Christmas, and she told me she might need to sell the house, which had been her childhood home, but she never told me she listed it with a realtor.

I parked my van and got her on the phone. "I told you I was going to put it up for sale," she said. Of course she did. But that was two months ago. I had no idea it would happen this soon. And I had no plan.

Before my divorce, I had been a homeschool mom who volunteered all the time. I never imagined I would become a single mom, so I stayed focused on raising my children. I knew how to manage their schedules, get them to their tutorial programs, acting gigs, rehearsals, auditions, gymnastics lessons, airsoft tournaments, art classes, theater performances. I taught them how to read and do basic math. I read to them ALL.THE.TIME.

I took on a few part-time gigs here and there as an actress or book editor, but the income from those things never amounted to much. As soon as word got out that I was getting a divorce, many of my friends said, "You're going to need to get a job." But I didn't want my kids to have to give up the life they knew, and, as my dear friend and fellow entrepreneur Carla White has often said, "I didn't want to outsource motherhood."

For 17 years, I spent my life volunteering my time with charitable organizations, nonprofits, churches, and arts organizations. I was a homeschool mom who read books to children.

I was no businesswoman.

I had to become one.

But I had NO IDEA where to begin.

I immediately started looking for alternative ways to make money while saying "yes" to almost anything that came along (including cleaning friends' houses). I needed to find something that I could do remotely, so I started looking online.

YouTube was full of ideas, but my signal would often drop while I was listening, and it was hard for me to get back to where I was if I lost my place. I also needed a platform that I could listen to instead of watch so I could multitask. That's when I discovered podcasts.

I started listening to business and marketing podcasts while I was driving (often for hours each day), making lunch, washing dishes, putting away laundry. Pretty much any time one of the kids wasn't talking to me (or singing at me).

As it turns out, podcasting would become the one thing to catapult me to business-owner status, but more on that later.

The first thing I had to do was secure a place to live that my kids and I couldn't get kicked out of. That was tough, considering I had no real income to show for the previous 17 years. Not many landlords want to rent to someone who can't prove they can afford to live there.

Thankfully, I had a rental house that I got in the divorce, and the renters happened to be moving out after two years of living there and paying rent consistently (which was how I was able to pay my own rent). I called one of my best friends, who was a real estate agent, and told her I needed to sell the house so I could have money to pay for a place to live.

Mandy helped me find a newly renovated house with the money from the sale of the rental house. There was only one problem. It was one-third of the size of my current house with less than a third of the yard. But it was low-maintenance. And it was close to my kids' dad's house. So I said, "YES."

Now, all of this was happening while I was helping a close friend take care of her boys as she fought stage 4 cancer. At the same time, I was going through perimenopause, so I was having hormonal surges, which led to hot flashes, night sweats, adult acne, and wave upon wave of anxiety. There were moments when I didn't think I was going to be able to stop crying.

I accidentally went on the divorce diet and lost 20 pounds. Even my dad, who never said much about me before, asked my mom if I was eating. He said I was starting to look bony. My friend Annie told me she was afraid to hug me too hard because it felt like I was going to break.

I almost did.

Living through an in-house separation had been almost unbearable. Months of co-existing in the same space while taking care of kids and losing one of my closest friends to cancer took a huge toll on my overall physical and mental health. Sleeping on a mattress on the floor in the renovated attic probably didn't help.

I can remember sitting up there with my laptop trying to learn marketable skills so I could support myself and my kids once the divorce was final. Somehow, in my search for "How to Make Money Online," I came across an email from OMG (One Man Gang).

I read several success stories from their students before I clicked on the link to watch the webinar. At the end of it, they had an endorsement from Bob Proctor who said to join. Of course, I said, "YES."

My introduction to Bob Proctor came a few years prior when Anne Kerry Ford, one of my mentors in network marketing (I never really made any money in direct sales, but I got a TON of personal development!), recommended that I read *It's Not About the Money* by Bob Proctor. I probably listened to it at least a dozen times.

One of the things he said that stuck with me was that you could take what you were making in a year and make it in a month. And you could take what you were making in a month and make it in a day.

The next step was trying to figure out how I was going to make that money.

I paid the coaching fee to OMG and took a deep dive into learning SEO (Search Engine Optimization). Holy smokes. Every time I tuned in for the training, I felt like I was being handed a technical manual written in Russian. And I don't speak Russian.

I'm not one to give up easily, though, so I kept tuning in and taking notes. When they started promoting an in-person event in the city where I lived, I said, "YES."

At OMG LIVE, I got to meet some of the biggest names in the digital marketing world, but I had no idea then how influential they were. I just knew that everyone seemed to be happy to connect, share ideas, speak the same language, and build each other up. It felt as though I had found my people.

When Kevin David, one of the speakers, mentioned that he was in the process of creating a course for people to learn how to build online courses, I had no idea what I was going to teach, but it sounded way easier than learning SEO, so I said, "YES."

Then, while sitting in the back of the room at the far left table, I noticed that the man to my right was about to get up to speak. He gave each one of us a copy of his book, *From the Trash Man to the Cash Man*. I took pages upon pages of notes (and later read them over and over again). The moment Myron Golden said the name of his mentor, Russell Brunson, I wrote it down. Because success leaves clues.

When I started listening to Russell's podcast, I discovered that he and his partner Todd Dickerson were going to be hosting a live event in Nashville, TN, just three months after the OMG LIVE event. In their online marketing, I saw that Myron would be one of the featured speakers.

Funnel Hacking Live 2019 was going to be held only 20 minutes from my house, and Myron Golden was going to be there. I felt like it would be ridiculous to say no. So, again, I said, "YES."

At that event, we were encouraged to write down the top 100 people we wanted to work with. At the very top of my list was Myron Golden. I wanted more than anything to help that man write his next book—

especially since I had read his first book to myself, read it aloud to my children twice, and read it to myself again.

My biggest YES probably happened when I read a quote on the back of a journal that Garrett J. White (one of the FHL speakers) gave to each of the attendees:

> "The **life** you want, the **marriage** you want, the
> **family** you want, is **fueled by** the **business** you're
> <u>**committed**</u> to build."

When I read that, I experienced unwavering belief. In my heart, I said, "YES, I believe that to be true." Then, I started acting as if it were true.

From there, I joined the 2CCX coaching program where I met other entrepreneurs on similar journeys. One of them had discovered a way to monetize his podcast. Since I had been listening to podcasts not only to keep my head above water but also to learn business and marketing, I decided to join his beta group. (Two more YESes!)

While I was learning how to create a professional and profitable podcast, I was in the middle of moving—as a single mom—with three kids. It was nuts. But I did it. I turned in all of the homework and ended up hitting "New and Noteworthy" on Apple Podcasts.

My podcast coach was always trying to help us find credible guests to interview, so when he said, "Hey, guys! Dan Henry just wrote his first book, and he normally doesn't do podcast interviews, but he's willing to do them as part of his book launch. Reach out to him!"

Easy enough, I thought. (I had no idea who Dan Henry was or why he was such a big deal. I just trusted my podcast coach and said, "YES.")

When I reached out to Dan on Facebook messenger, I said, "Hey, Dan, our mutual friend Jamie Atkinson suggested that I reach out to you as an excellent guest for my podcast. He says you have a book you're trying to promote, and I am absolutely on board with that."

He wrote back, "Hey there! I don't normally do podcasts, but I'm going to do a podcast tour soon to promote my book. If you give me a name and email, I'll put you on my list and reach out when I'm ready."

I gave him my contact information and then said, "Congratulations on writing and publishing a book! I'm a book editor, so I know what a grueling process it can be. HUGE WIN!"

To which he said, "Oh awesome! Maybe I should hire you for the edit haha."

I basically told him, "Yes, you should!" After I explained that I had a reputation for polishing self-published books so they didn't look self-published, he agreed to hire me. But he said he needed it done in a few weeks. He was going to be speaking at FHL 2020 and he had hoped to give away a copy to everyone who attended.

It was a race to the finish line, but we made it! His book—which included my name in the acknowledgments—was placed in every seat in the house when he took the stage to speak.

And the rest, as they say, is history. Dan Henry's *Digital Millionaire Secrets* went on to become not only an international bestseller but also hit #3 in all of Amazon Kindle. It is now a *USA Today* and *Wall Street Journal* bestseller. He was so pleased with the process and the product that he started recommending me to all of his super-performer friends, including Ryan Stewman, who wrote the foreword for this book.

Dan's book foreword was written by Myron Golden, which means I had a reason to reach out to Myron. After I worked my magic on

Myron's foreword, he read it and said, "Lori, you are a phenomenal editor, and I will have to do some work with you moving forward." I was one step closer to helping Myron write his next book!

When Dan held a high-level mastermind a few months later and spent a weekend teaching his clients how to write and market a bestselling book to build a business, he had me speak to them. Then, he told them that they all needed to write a book, and if they wanted it to be as good as his, they needed to hire me as their editor. The moment he told them to put down a $1,000 deposit with me, I made $15,000 in 15 minutes. It was unreal.

For context, the previous year, I lived on less than $36,000. If you divide that up among four people (my three kids and me), that's less than $10,000 per person for the entire year.

All of a sudden, my book editing business was booked out for 2020.

I decided to hire a bookkeeper to help me keep track of my income and expenses, and at the end of the year, I hit the 6-figure mark. It took years for my kids' dad to achieve 6-figure status as an employee, but I managed to do it in a single year as an entrepreneur.

Then, in July 2021, my book editing dream came true. Myron Golden approached me about helping him write his next book. I was THRILLED. Thanks to glowing recommendations from Dan, Ryan, and now Myron, I had not only one but THREE books in seats at FHL 2021: *B.O.S.S. Moves* by Myron Golden, *One Day Cash Machine* by Eileen Wilder, and *Million Dollar Family Secrets* by Kiana Danial (which made it to #10 in all of Amazon Kindle and hit the *USA Today* and *Wall Street Journal* bestseller lists).

Looking back, I can see the path, but at the beginning, I had NO IDEA how that path would unfold. I just kept following those inner nudges and saying, "YES." And I kept saying, "YES." That's the one thing that

I know led me from feeling like Cinderella in the attic to becoming a 6-figure business owner.

If I hadn't said yes to joining my friend's network marketing opportunity back in February 2015, I never would have read Bob Proctor's book, and I never would have joined OMG, which means I never would have met Myron Golden or started listening to Russell Brunson's podcast or met Dan Henry who introduced me to Shanda Trofe, the design ninja behind almost every book I edit.

I also never would have attended Funnel Hacking Live 2019, where I met my future coauthor and business partner Timothy R. Johnson, who has helped me scale my book-editing business. If I hadn't scaled, I never would have put out a call for proofreaders and editors, which is how I found my DragonflyWings.Ink partner Shelby Rawson and my dream team, including Mary Rembert, Clare Fernandez, and Kathy Haskins.

I certainly wouldn't have connected with brilliant minds like Ariel Amavi, Ron Cool, Cory Carter, or Josh Forti, who have been instrumental in helping me structure my Boss Authors Mastermind (BAM). As the adage goes, there's no such thing as self-made millionaires, only team-made millionaires.

On a personal note, remember that quote I read at FHL 2019 about "the marriage you want"? Well, at the end of 2021, one of my authors, a man who captured my heart and the heart of my children—a brilliant and beautiful soul by the name of Anthony S. Blair—asked me to marry him. And I said, "YES."

Ant Blair came to me through the recommendation of another one of my authors, Jeff Wickersham. Jeff and I met inside of a mastermind group that I joined at the urging of Russell Brunson. Making business connections matters. It also helps if you pay to play because as Russell says, "People who pay, pay attention."

A Million Dollar Identity is much easier to attain when you're surrounded by people who are all high achievers, peak performers, and top income earners. Becoming a published author is the fastest way to increase your authority ("author" is the root word for "authority"). Most business owners are great communicators but terrible writers. A professional editor can bridge that gap.

I've received messy transcriptions from coaches who know how to make money with their mouths but can't spell to save their lives. They have great ideas but have trouble getting them down on paper for other people to read. My company translates gobbledygook into compelling books that people will read, review, and recommend. Our favorite reviewers say, "I hadn't read a book in years, but I couldn't put this one down," and, "This book changed my life!"

If you're an aspiring self-published author who needs help navigating the writing process from inception to creation to market domination, then your next step is to grab my basic book framework at the link below, and keep saying, "YES."

BossAuthors.com

CHAPTER EIGHTEEN

ANGELA LITTLE

Angela Little

Angela Little is the CEO of Million Dollars Mastermind, a Million Dollar Story Agency partner, and a single mom of four kids. As a former competitive bodybuilder, she holds the titles of Female Overall European Pro Champion and both European and British bikini bodybuilding champion. She is a fierce advocate of women's rights and passionate about health biohacking, believing that when we combine the right business strategy, the correct mindset, and physical health, we can achieve EVERYTHING. With a strong marketing, communications, and business background, combined with decades of experience in health and beauty, her purpose is to help fellow entrepreneurs develop and grow their business, coaching them through the Million Dollars Mastermind, which combines systems and strategies with a growth mindset.

LIFE WITHOUT LIMITS

There was something profound about the possession order for my nightclub coming through on the day of my birthday. I remember it so well … It was my 40th. *Why on earth had I done it?* I had been doing well before.

I had three successful businesses and then chose to sell them to put everything into a business that I didn't know or understand. It seems crazy thinking about it now.

I believed I had the Midas touch, and everything I did turned to gold, but I had taken a huge risk at a time when I was raising three young kids and in a very unstable relationship! Had my ego gotten the better of me?

For the outside world, I always put on a brave face. After all, I had young children, and I had to be a good role model and show strength. And, well, I'm English, and that's what we do. We pretend everything is "just fine." The reality was that I was far from fine.

I think I cried every single night for at least eight months—obviously in private when no one could hear me. I cried because I'd invested twenty years trying to please someone who only found fault with me and because I had zero money after losing the nightclub.

With young mouths to feed and children with additional needs, I wandered around in a haze, not knowing what to do. It was easy to take over the role of putting myself down, even after he had left. Saving myself emotionally and financially felt like an impossible task!

What's this? I thought, *Is this going to be MY story? Broken, broke single mom, tens of thousands of pounds in debt, without a single asset to my name, no way to get credit, living off benefits ... What was I going to do to dig myself out of this hole?*

I knew I had to start again. I knew I had to sort my head out.

I had so many ambitions and dreams of how my life would be. *How on earth was I going to go on from here?*

One day, when I was at my lowest ebb, I remembered that I had collected lots of motivational videos for my older son because I understood his Thai boxing was a mental game, not merely a physical one. I began listening to them myself, and that's when I found Tony Robbins.

Listening to Tony's teachings became my new obsession. I had him on repeat. I bathed in his words, listening to him day and night, on my walks, and while I relaxed in a hot bath. All the while, I was reminded of the strength hiding inside me, feeling and knowing I could do better, knowing I was worth more. I just had to remember how to believe in myself again because I knew I was done for if I fed the beast of my inner critic.

And I had no intention of living my life that way.

I decided to go to one of Tony's events even though I wasn't sure how to pull it off since most of his events are held in America, and the kids and I were still in a bad way financially. But I knew that to flourish in life, to find happiness and joy, I had to invest somehow in self-care.

To my surprise, Tony Robbins came to the UK in April the following year. I didn't know how exactly, but I was going to get there! I would rub elbows with like-minded people, walk on fire, and regain my strength. I would cry, scream, let it all out, and have a deeply cleansing experience. I knew I couldn't afford a ticket, but I was also certain that my life depended on getting one.

Every day, I would check forums, looking for a ticket. Then, after Christmas, my opportunity arose. Someone was selling a ticket for £200. Jackpot! I was going! Fate had stepped in.

There was a massive queue in London at the event, and as we all piled in the doors, we were excited by such a buzz. The energy in the room was electric. I was so ecstatic about being with these people. 5,000 of MY people. I was filled with love and hope for a new beginning. We all knew what was going to happen. Every person would cry and heal and make new friends in the process! We all wanted to "unleash the power within" where the impossible becomes possible. That resonated with me.

I talked about my struggles and opened up about my hopes and dreams for the future. I learned that you have to look inside yourself to discover how you feel about yourself. You can't make good decisions if you don't trust yourself. When I returned from the Tony Robbins event, I delved into self-healing to learn to love myself again. I meditated every day and was able to begin to process my thoughts and how I reacted. I became a master of my soul. I consumed every book I could find about meditation, self-talk, habits, happiness, and inner peace. I knew my *future self* depended on my dedication to this journey.

I began to understand that my destiny was in my own hands and no one else's. I have a huge heart and a tremendous entrepreneurial spirit, and I decided that mastering the online digital space was the key to my future success.

I also know that to give your best self to you and others, you have to look after your body as well as your mindset. You must treat the beautiful machine (your body) that you have been blessed with as one

of the most precious things in your life. An analogy I use is from the great Warren Buffet. He says you get to choose one car, one beautiful, shiny, fantastic car. The only catch is that it's yours for the rest of your life, and you do not get another one. How would you treat that car?

You would give it the best oil and fuel and always make sure it's clean, shiny, looked after, and loved with new tires because you know that you could never replace it, and you want it to always be the best. This is how you have to treat your body. You have to do the work so that your body functions properly.

There's nothing better than feeling strong in my body. I lift weights, and I love it. It makes my mind feel strong and my body feel and function the way it was designed to. My mental strength radiates from my physical strength. When these strengths are aligned, they work as one.

I am a mom who wants to play all-out. I do not want to be a mom who can't keep up with her children. My children have told me they expect me to live to be 100, and as far as I'm concerned, it's my absolute intent to respect their wishes!

After attending Tony Robbins, and as part of my healing journey, I decided to do a bikini competition. I found a coach and slowly I started losing body fat. At first, I had to force myself. My coach gave me a plan that I followed daily, even if I didn't feel like it. Training for the competition was much like running a business; being disciplined and consistent takes the win. I whipped my worn-out, wonderful body that had given birth to four kiddos into shape and acknowledged that you have to invest in yourself to truly *be* yourself.

There are a lot of entrepreneurs who take weight training and fitness biohacking to a whole new level. They know this is an essential part of who they are, how they want to be seen, and how they show up in the world. They know that when the body is aligned with their brain and mental strength, they make good decisions. And I think this, too.

I did exactly what I was told to do and trusted my coach. And as I started losing weight, I started getting to know my authentic self again—someone I had lost under the pressure I put myself through for failing. One key to lasting success is learning not to beat yourself up.

Now, you might think a bodybuilding show is only about your body. Oh ... no, no, no. Competitors challenge themselves; it's a mental strength game. I mean, there is nothing more reassuring than knowing that your body and your mind can work in harmony. In turn, learning to trust my instincts has affected what I do personally and in business which has completely changed my world over the last few years. I've become *confident and competent*. If something doesn't go to plan, it's how it is meant to be. I take it as a lesson that, even though I might not know why *yet*, I will at some point understand why it happened.

So, how do you want to show up?

What does success look like to you?

Is it financial?

It's ok if it is. I always dreamed I would be incredibly wealthy, and there's nothing wrong with that.

We are often told that our "why" has to be for other people. It's good to help others, but *you have to help yourself first, my friend*. Otherwise, you are stuck. And how long have you been stuck?

Success to you might be to buy back time and have more freedom. It might mean helping your parents or your children.

Today I fully trust myself. I have zero reservations about who I am as a person. I have a blessed life filled with joy and thrilling adventures. I have four exceptional children, and this year I became a grandma. They bring so much fun and love to my life.

When I was at rock bottom, I had no idea how I was ever going to break through. Living day by day, I felt invisible, lost, and unloved. I want you to know if that's you right now, I understand it feels complex and impossible, but I promise you that you will succeed and feel better with the proper guidance. Each day can move you one step forward. There is light and love and happiness at the end of the road. You simply have to open yourself up to it.

Remember this one important thing. You cannot move forward alone. We all need support and a guide to show us the shortcuts, encourage us, and help us be our best selves. You have to create a machine that drives awareness to you and to what you do. Nothing will stop you from reaching your goals with your newfound growth mindset, self-belief, and strength.

In our mastermind, we help entrepreneurs become the people they always believed they could be. We want you to dream big, and we'll help you apply business strategy so you succeed.

The very first thing I teach is to get to "know thyself." If you can honestly know who you are and be your authentic self, you can accept yourself and teach your clients from the heart.

"Life Without Limits" (as you've probably guessed from the title of my chapter) is something I often say and strongly believe in. I love that saying so much I have it tattooed on me. It's one sentence that tells you who I am and what I think. I don't hold back, and I want this for you, too. I give life everything, and I want everybody to experience how amazing that feels.

To everybody I know and everybody I don't know - *Do not put limits on your life! You have the power and control over yourself, and only you can stand in your way!*

Now, I'm doing exactly what I am meant to be doing. I go to events, I have a growth mindset, and I mix with like-minded entrepreneurs.

My business partner, Jamie Wolf, and I run a successful publishing and marketing company plus an online education company that offers group coaching. We help business owners and entrepreneurs craft their high-ticket offers and produce a book. Business owners who write books open up their world to potential speaking gigs. They get booked on podcasts. And they get taken seriously when people come into their world.

Their prospective clients get to know, like, and trust them simply by reading their book, which compresses the time it would typically take for a lead to move from being cold traffic to warm traffic (from a perfect stranger to a potential customer).

When prospective clients feel fully aligned with an author or speaker, they want to enter that influencer's world and work with them. It's that simple.

This is what we help entrepreneurs and professionals do. We help them get their message out.

Jamie and I take our clients on a journey, helping them discover who they are, what they offer, and what they're known for. We find out their goals, their struggles, and what success looks like to them, and we give them the tools to accomplish that and more!

We help entrepreneurs express themselves to become authentic in their coaching programs. We help them create their platform and get all their assets created so they can go out into the world and deliver more value than ever before.

When they experience the reward of giving to others, they can't help but feel good about the career they've created and the life they've built for their family, for their clients, and ultimately for their clients' families.

We desire to help entrepreneurs create the life they've always dreamed of but didn't believe was possible.

If that sounds like you, then we want to help you take your business to six-, seven-, eight-, even nine-figures, and more, having that hot body and that joyful, restful brain filled with gratitude. And I am confident that we have the knowledge to do this *for* you and *with* you.

If you're stuck, I understand. I have been there, too. But now I have the answer. I have the road map. I've done all the hard work for you, and I can help you take your business to the next level.

But first, we have to find out who you are, what your goals are, what you want to accomplish, and what you can offer your audience. We help you get to know yourself, find your true purpose, and make money along the way.

Do not ever be afraid of claiming you want to build generational wealth. So many people are scared to say that they have financial goals, want to be rich, or want to be wealthy. But they still have a purpose— they have perfect purpose and profit *together*. And why shouldn't you?

You are designed to live an extraordinary life with purpose. To help yourself first. To then lead your family, your circle, and your community. But you can only do these things if you are making a profit.

We want you to get paid so well that you can have everything you want. If that's what is in your heart, know that you can have it. Come with us and let's make success happen together:

MillionDollarsMastermind.com

CHAPTER NINETEEN

JAMES GOLDEN

James Golden

James Golden is the Founder and CEO of both the Pavement Management Group and JG3 Consulting, LLC. At nineteen, he began his career and ventured into business, consulting, and entrepreneurship. That led him into a twenty-three-year career and calling for helping municipalities throughout the U.S. If you're looking for a roadway preservation advocate, James is your man. You can also find James encouraging others to be the best version of themselves through his *Good to Goalden* podcast, as well as his personal and group coaching with The Goalden Collective.

THE ROAD TO LEVEL UP
IS PAVED IN GOALD

"Beep, Beep, Beep, Beep, Beep, Beep ... I can do this all morning!" screams Dwayne "The Rock" Johnson.

"Hey, can you please tell The Rock to shut the eff up?!"

And there she is, the beauty *and* the beast ... right on point and right on time with her southern charm! Even though my initial reaction is to be pissed off, deep down, her sarcasm and ability to call me out on my shit is one of the most attractive things about her. That's why I married her!

I rise, silence the pleas from The Rock and my wife, and slowly prepare myself for the daily grind ahead. I'm about to do a deep dive with guys who are in the same shoes I was in ten years ago. It looked something like this ...

Another day of managing both a career and family that had lost their confidence in me. Thirty-day stints of personal development and goal setting paired with some gym check-ins and a few podcast downloads. I was all talk, no action.

My boss saw it, my coworkers saw it, my wife saw it, and worst of all, my kids saw it. Every year was the same. Year after year of living life at the same level of health, wealth, relationships, cars, vacations, etc., for me and the fam.

Even though I was a high performer, had a combined six-figure income, and my family was taken care of, there was something profound inside of me telling me that I could do better. Unfortunately, I struggled to find the GPS for the success I was looking for, and motivational content had lost its luster.

Meanwhile, my wife, kids, social media feed, co-workers, and friends seemed perfectly content. Everyone around me seemed content with complaining about politics, gossiping about one another, being overweight, bingeing Netflix at night and on weekends, still hanging out at the bars, and living paycheck to paycheck.

I dreamed of a lifestyle in which I had freedom from the stresses of a typical 9-5 grind while running a successful company and providing the gift of time and experiences with my wife and family—not a mountain of debt, false hope, and false promises.

After working hard at a startup company for over thirteen years, I became the Chief Operating Officer. We had nice cars, took nice vacations with our three kids and friends, hosted many parties at our brand new home in the best neighborhood in town, and appeared to be living the American dream.

The problem was that we resented each other, took a lot of it out on the kids, racked up tens of thousands in credit card charges to continue supporting our lifestyle, and faked our way through love and happiness day in and day out. To make matters worse, my mentor and boss scheduled me for a meeting on December 28 at the offices with HR, which probably tells you everything you need to know.

I walked out of the office that day with the weight of the world on my shoulders. Half of me was scared to death about going home to tell my wife that my career and our cash flow were gone. The other half saw this as a "Goalden" opportunity to transition from intrapreneur to entrepreneur and start my own firm! And I did just that.

Little did I know that a single event of losing my job would set the stage for a complete, life-altering change! Within a single calendar year in 2011, I lost my career, started my first company, my wife left, I became a weekend dad, I lost my house, and I moved back into my parent's basement, starting all over again at the age of 33 years old.

The struggle was real, and the amount of pressure I felt would go one of two ways.

Despite several weeks of feeling empty and alone, a higher power was knocking on my door, and fortunately, I was eager and willing to listen. As I look back on those times, I am nothing but grateful. Those learning experiences were worth their weight in gold and led me to build a company and life I am incredibly proud of.

I listened to motivational quotes and attended self-help help seminars for years, but without action, all that personal development was a fast track to nowhere. I discovered that the only way to move the needle forward was to silence the voices inside telling me it was okay to continue living an average life of comfort.

Lack of action feeds imposter syndrome, putting you into a constant state of feeling stuck and comfortable, and the only one powerful enough to change this is *you*.

I have been in those exact shoes, and I know all the associated feelings … the anxiety, the stress, the pressure, and the fear. I can recount many dark days of sitting alone in a room of silence, yet the chatter of failure, disappointment, and depression was louder than a freight train.

On one of these occasions, I was out of town for business and alone in a hotel room, putting back my third or fourth Budweiser. I cracked open my laptop and found myself on Amazon.com, entering "leader-ship books" into the search bar.

That is when I found and purchased my first book ever. A book that taught me that no one was coming to save me. If I wanted to lead a life by design, it was up to me to hold myself accountable, change my environment, become a leader, let go of the things I couldn't control, and get to work. The book was *Extreme Ownership: How U.S. Navy SEALS Lead and Win* by Jocko Willink and Leif Babin.

This book served as the catalyst of change, providing me with instructional mindset and tactics, lighting a fire within to learn more. After completing it, I purchased more physical books and then discovered Audible for listening to books while traveling.

Audible became a game-changer and allowed me to maximize my downtime when driving or flying. Shortly after, I discovered podcasts, which ultimately led me to my current network affiliations, creating business connections across the country.

Usually, I would turn up the volume in my car on some 90's gangsta rap, but one day, during a seemingly benign Starbucks run, the "Episodes for You" section of my Spotify caught my attention. That day, the universe had other plans for me as a particular podcast called *ReWire* from some guy named Ryan Stewman started to play.

I thought to myself, *Who the eff is this guy?* Then, I tapped the podcast icon, turned up the volume, and made my way to Starbucks. (In case you skipped the foreword to this book, Ryan is the guy who wrote it. He has since become my mentor and friend.)

Since those defining moments, my life has never been the same.

The greatest blessing, in the midst of all that chaos, has been finding my true soul mate. She has always supported me to chase my dreams while managing to keep me in check on what matters most in this life of ours—our family.

If there's one thing I've found in my eleven years of owning a business, it's that there are no shortcuts along the journey to success. The roads you'll travel will be full of potholes, wrong turns, dead-ends, and pit stops, appearing out of nowhere just as you think you've got something figured out or are gaining momentum.

To make matters worse, you are entering uncharted territory amongst your now-former co-workers, your family members, and friends. How will they react to Mr. Bigshot over there, losing his comfortable and reliable job and starting a business? I know that you don't want anything within your relationships and circle to change, but the fact is everything will change.

When you reject the force of average and eliminate excuses from your vocabulary, your perception of just about everything will change. All of a sudden, grabbing beers on a Monday night to watch the football game with your friends is no longer a priority. You'd rather stick to your healthy diet, plan your schedule for the next day, and get up at 5 a.m. to get that workout in.

Great leaders think with a winning mindset, practice extreme owner-ship, and focus on chasing greatness. Think about your friends and family for a minute. Can you honestly say they will all support your new initiative? Unfortunately, the answer is no. You've got some tough decisions to make, and you need to make them ASAP.

I can tell you it's hard, and I mean really hard. Fortunately, the people that do matter most will stick by you, or after a long enough period, will reappear, support you, and look to you as a leader. Now that's some real talk right there! But on day one, that's the farthest thing from your mind.

You are guaranteed to lose support along the way, and I want you to realize that this is okay! It's similar to a snake that sheds its skin. It's a part of the growth process, and the easiest way to do it is by just ripping the bandage off. Stop attending functions and associating with those around you who are not adding value to you and your family's life.

By now, I'm sure you've heard that you are the average of the five people you spend most of your time with. You're probably even thinking about your shortlist of friends, your family members, your parents, the couples you and your partner hang out with, and the parents on the sidelines of your kid's soccer games that you see more than you'd like to.

How many are you excited to be around, have a conversation with, and talk about leveling up with? If you were anything like me when I went through this exercise, the answer was two. So go ahead, pick your top five, think about yourself right now and ask yourself, are you the average of these five people?

If you answered yes, and it scares you, *then good.* You are right where you need to be at this point. Suppose you said no, because you are on a completely different track, then good. You are right where you need to be at this point, as well.

The bottom line is that the level-up and business ownership game can be a rocky and lonely journey. The only real magical solution and shortcut to hitting the next level in all areas of your life is to stop trying to go it alone! One of my sayings is, "find your tribe, or build your tribe, or better yet, do both!" Either way, you need to surround yourself with people who possess a winning mindset—*NO*, a GOALDEN mindset.

Those who take action with intent, purpose, and passion recognize failure as nothing more than a step in the right direction. There are no excuses, and the only way to move forward is through leadership and extreme ownership while in pursuit of hitting the next goal.

I can tell you that it wasn't until seven years into my journey that I found the tribe. Here we are ten years later, and I am building my own business and have achieved levels of success I could have once only dreamed about.

It's truly unique what happens when you get the right people into the right circle and at the right time. The GOALDEN mindset is infectious and forces you to think in ways you have never considered before. It's time to step outside of your comfort zone and step into greatness by finding a like-minded band of brothers and sisters whose mission resonates with yours.

There are levels to EVERYTHING in life, from your finances, business holdings, relationships, the way you fly, what you drive and where you park, the type of mindset you have, your physique, and overall health. To create a Million Dollar Mindset, you need to envision yourself on a mission to start the business that will catapult you to become the best version of yourself. To get there, you're probably going to need some help!

After all, what good is becoming a millionaire if your relationships are horrible, your mindset is broken, and your health is in jeopardy because you're overweight?

The success journey is full of risks, and this trip requires a level head, a strong stomach, and an unbreakable will. After all, nobody said this was going to be easy. If it were, the world would be full of high-level operators working to become the most excellent version of themselves by constantly leveling up!

The reality is that only the top 1% hold this mission, and since you are still with me, I'd like to congratulate you on being in that group and personally welcome you to The Goalden Collective.

The Goalden Collective

The Goalden Collective is a group dedicated to goal-oriented high performers committed to living by the Golden Rule. It's perfect for those looking to rip the bandage off of their old life, step outside their comfort zone, and join some like-minded individuals. It serves as a starting point for community and networking and will be essential to chase greatness.

The Goald Mine

The Goald Mine membership extends from and serves the Goalden Collective. Members receive resources, weekly actionable content, mentorship, challenges, and accountability from hand-selected Goalden Mentors. These mentors are recognized experts within their field and guide the group in defining and hitting their next levels in all aspects of the success journey. The Goald Mine currently has a cap of 100 members to best serve the needs of the group.

Good to Goalden Mastermind

Good to Goalden is designed to get you on the fast track to a passionate, fulfilled life at home while working to realize your Million Dollar Identity and 7-figure revenues! To best serve the needs of my one-on-one clients and be able to go all-in alongside them on their journey, this opportunity is only available to four success-driven individuals at a time.

Goalden Initiative

Three years ago, I made it a mission first to find my tribe and then build my tribe of like-minded individuals. The Goalden Collective, Goald Mine, and Good to Goalden Mastermind are all part of the Goalden Initiative, which I've created because these options were not available to me when I first started entrepreneurship.

If you are anything like me, your greatest fear is the fear of being average. Let me help you solve that by joining the Goalden Initiative today through any of the three Goalden Opportunities available by visiting:

GoaldenConsulting.com

CHAPTER TWENTY

ARIEL AMAVI

Ariel Amavi

Ariel Amavi has worked with some of the top internet marketers on the planet, providing international consulting services to over 100 companies. She works with pro teams, celebrities, athletes, and titans of industry such as Russell Brunson, Alex Charfen, Myron Golden, and many more. She's had a 7-figure exit, helped broker multiple business deals ranging from $50K to $3B, and lived and worked in eight different countries.

Ariel is the creator of the H.E.A.L. Method™. She has created, patented, manufactured, and brought to market Automated Resistance Training™ exercise equipment. She served as CMO for a nonprofit to solve food insecurity. She also designed and manufactured a backpack to save orphans. She helped start a concierge medical practice and developed mobile fitness and corporate wellness programs.

Featured on FOX News and in John Little's book *The Time-Savers Workout*, she has appeared on Funnel Hacker TV and spoken on various summits and podcasts.

ACTIVATE YOUR INNER SUPER PERFORMER

Walking through Home Depot, I was pushing a cart with a slightly creaky wheel when I noticed a man approaching from the other end of the aisle. My heart began to beat faster. I suddenly felt tension in my body. Immediately, I started scanning the shelves, looking for something I could use either as a weapon or a shield. *Was anyone else nearby? How far away was the door?*

That was the moment everything changed.

Leading up to that moment, I had spent years boxing, fighting MMA, and learning self-defense after being sexually assaulted in my early 20s. I learned the skills to protect myself, so I was ready. Always ready. That day at Home Depot was a turning point. I was no longer willing to view everyone and everything around me as a threat. I was fed up with being in a constant state of fight or flight. It was time to let go of that identity.

In the process of all of the fighting, I had become a professional at wrecking my body. When I stopped fighting and decided to create a new life for myself, I also decided it was time for a career change.

All of the damage to my body had allowed me to meet a lot of wellness practitioners, and I loved the idea of helping them increase their impact. I started a coaching and consulting business to help wellness providers grow and scale. Ironically, before I knew it, I had gained almost 100 lbs, and my health was deteriorating.

Even though I was no longer fighting, I was still fiercely competitive. I would go to the gym and be super pumped, but I would go too hard.

Then, I would hurt too much to return the next day. Sometimes I would push myself to go back and fight through the pain, but that always made it worse.

Pushing myself wasn't restricted to the gym either. I'd start a new diet, go all in, and eventually fall off the wagon within a few days. It seemed like the cycle would never end.

Despite all of my physical challenges, my business was going great. I was working with some of the top entrepreneurs and titans of industry, yet I couldn't get my body on track. My weight, energy, and self-esteem were like a yo-yo. Up and down, up and down.

I decided to look for the leverage points. I dug deep. Reading research studies, examining different technologies, and exploring training methods. As I began to understand the human body, I decided to acquire some of these technologies and their intellectual property. I brought in the right people and new concepts, and together, we created a device that compressed exercise time from 5 to 7 hours per week down to *10 minutes per week* while achieving better results. Yes, per week. That is the power of leverage.

Everything I was doing for my clients was helping them understand leverage and how to minimize their input while maximizing their output. It occurred to me that I simply needed to use that concept to create a new approach for myself.

First, I looked at people in peak physical condition. Then I studied high-income earners. Professional athletes are both—they earn millions of dollars and, for the most part, are in great health. I started watching for patterns. I noticed that super performers spend a lot of time and money taking care of their bodies.

Then, I looked at entrepreneurs who were either earning or wanting to earn millions of dollars. I wanted to know what separated the super successful from the moderately successful. I started to find that the less successful entrepreneurs tend to work long hours, spend a lot of time in front of a screen, sacrifice sleep, and skip meals more often than not. They weren't exactly taking care of their bodies.

The super performers were the ones who were activated. They were engaged in caring for their bodies as if they were professional athletes. It made all the difference.

I knew then if I wanted to take control of my life, I had to leverage my body.

One day it occurred to me that the human body is the most astonishing machine on this planet. It is constantly adapting and evolving. If we were just beings floating around without bodies, and then, suddenly, we were given one of these meat suits to drive around, we would likely think it was the coolest thing ever.

You can cut it, and it will heal. You can eat just about anything, and it will find a way to turn it into fuel. It will let you feel anything you can imagine—the breeze on your skin, the sun on your face, the touch of a loved one. Pleasure, pain, energy, fatigue … You can experience it all with the human body.

The human body is absolutely amazing. It gives whatever it is primed for. The best part is also the worst part: It's absolutely free. It's a gift every human is born with, so many of us take it for granted.

What if you had to buy your body? What if your body was the price of a luxury car? Would you use premium fuel and keep it clean? Would you try to prevent it from getting scratched or dented? If your luxury car cost $100K (or more), would you treat it like you got it for free?

Your body is a critical piece of you being able to earn millions of dollars, but it was free. Because it has always supported you without your awareness, it's easy to neglect it and overlook how much ROI you can get from caring for it.

Your body is the strongest and most important lever you will ever encounter. If you want to maximize the possibilities for leverage in your business, you have to start with your body. When you activate this giant lever, your business and everything else in your life will flow with ease. Activations are small inputs that create big outputs.

I began to recognize that most coaching programs don't work because they're created for average performers. High performers make programs for average performers to do slightly better, and there is a massive gap between super performers and everyone else.

Super performers are activated. They work smarter, not harder. They understand how to leverage their body, their mind, their energy, and their time. Therefore, their business—and their entire life—benefits. Super performers exchange the hustle and grind for daily activations that are simple and incredibly effective.

The following series of activations have the power to significantly change your life. They are completely free and will help you start to leverage your physical body so you can do, be, give, and have *more*. You can access the activations and resources explaining how/why these methods work so well by using the website at the end of this chapter.

These few simple steps will help you leverage your body and your mind:

Hydration

If you drink 30 ounces of water within 30 minutes of waking up, you leverage everything in your body. The simple act of hydration wakes up your metabolism and sends your cells a signal that says you are in a place of abundance. With that trigger, they begin to release the things they do not need and work more effectively and efficiently.

As for the rest of the day, when you think about water, drink more. If you think about it at all, drink up. Even if the thought is along the lines of how much more frequently you're using the restroom, grab some more water and drink. Your body will tell you how much water it needs. It is also important to note that the quality of water you consume matters.

Movement

This may come as a shock, but our bodies are actually created for movement. If you're thinking that walking from the couch to the kitchen counts, then you probably need to stretch that idea a bit (though I've been guilty of moving that little, too).

We talk all the time about movement and exercise and going to the gym, but it doesn't have to be that complicated. Just get moving. I don't care if you do jumping jacks, push-ups, burpees, go for a walk, wrestle with your kids, go up and down the stairs a few times, dance, or run a freaking marathon, just MOVE YOUR BODY.

The goal is to move all of your body and get your heart rate up.

Obviously, the more you move, the faster you move, the better your overall health benefits will be, but in order to properly leverage your life, you simply need to find the way you like best to move and commit to it. Just start there.

Half the problem most people run into is that they make movement and exercise a complicated process. Don't get me wrong, I'm all for getting a crazy-good workout in, but it's not always going to happen.

To recap, the first part of leverage in movement is just to simply get moving. Now, let's take it to the next level. To really maximize the benefits from your movement, lift some weights. This doesn't have to be complicated, and you don't need many lifts, just a few movements and some resistance will make a HUGE change in your body over time. As with all things fitness, not all exercises or reps are created equal.

A word of caution: Do not separate body parts for days of the week. In other words, don't subscribe to the old notion of leg day, chest and back day, etc. When people tell me they do this, I simply ask one question: On leg day, when you wake up in the morning and you drink your water, do you tell your body, "Hey, it's leg day, so only the legs get this water"? No? That's because **everything we do with our body we do for our entire body.** We eat, sleep, and drink for our entire body.

If everything we do is for the entire body, then why do we take a different approach for exercise?

I think there are a couple of reasons for this.

First, we have created a multi-trillion dollar industry out of complicating the one thing that every consumer on the planet has—a body. We all have one in some form or another, and anyone who stands to profit from our dissatisfaction with our body makes it a point to make everything seem complicated. Don't get me wrong, the body is a complex and amazing machine, but maintaining it isn't exactly rocket science.

Second, we work out improperly. This is likely due to thinking we have to overcomplicate our workouts. This leads to injury, lack of results, and burnout. (Kinda sounds like business sometimes, doesn't it?)

We split up our efforts to target different parts of the body because we are attempting to force results that would come naturally if we simply paid attention to the points of leverage.

In order to maximize your movement, you only need to do a few things.

1. Massively load your quads and glutes.

2. Move slowly under load.

3. Actively stretch.

4. Focus on breathing.

Massively Load Your Quads and Glutes

Without taking you too far into the weeds on why this is so important, consider this: In the past, human survival was dependent upon our ability to either outrun predators or run down prey.

Outside of our heart and lungs, our body prioritizes our legs. When we deplete the energy stores in our legs, our body rapidly replenishes them. It does this by drawing from everywhere else in the body. The liver goes into overdrive, and cells start dumping resources.

Leg presses, lunges, and squats are all awesome for this, giving an incredible boost for the body. All you have to do is push yourself to failure. What I mean by that is go until you can't go anymore.

Don't stop when your brain says you're done. Stop when your legs say they're done. I want you to shake and feel weak and push through it.

For example, hold a wall squat until your legs give out. Or do walking lunges until you dip down and can't lift yourself again. Then stop. Take a breath and a 15- to 30-second break, then try again.

Your body will start repairing your legs in milliseconds.

Try another round and go until you can't. Then you're done. You can do this in a few minutes if you push yourself.

Wall squats are my number one activation to get rid of anxiety and relieve stress.

Move Slowly Under Load

When people lift weights, they tend to use momentum to move the weight instead of actually using the required muscles. When we rely on speed to get from Point A to Point B during a repetition, we don't really get the same benefit as if we were to control the entire motion (the same principle applies in business, by the way).

First, select the right weight (more on that in a moment). Then, move slowly and steadily until you are fatigued.

For example, look at a bicep curl. Starting with your arm to the side, bent at 90 degrees so your hand is in front of you, think of what would happen if you were to place a weight in your hand. One of three things will occur:

1. The weight will force your hand down toward the ground. This represents **over-load.**

2. You will be able to lift the weight, bringing your hand upward toward your shoulder. This represents **under-load.**

3. You will struggle to do so, but your hand can remain where it is with the weight, unable to lift but able to resist lowering. This represents **perfect-load**.

As you can imagine, perfect-load doesn't exist in the gym. Even if it did, it would only apply to that one spot in the range of motion. If you were to lift or lower your arm a single degree, that load would need to change because your capability would change.

I could spend a few thousand words dissecting and explaining the how and why, so if you're interested, check out the link at the end of this chapter.

Since perfect-load is nearly impossible, that leaves us with being either under- or over-load. Over-load is where we get injured. We don't want that. So we have to find the right amount of weight that will be challenging while still safe to move. Essentially, you need to be able to lift the weight, but it should be challenging enough so that you can only do it a few times before feeling fatigued. Just like with the wall squats, push yourself to failure.

Actively Stretch

For years we have been taught to stretch as far as we can and to hold for 30 seconds or so. This is another area where I could talk for a long time, but I'll skip to the point and tell you the key to effectively stretching any muscle. This method will drastically improve your flexibility and the way your entire body feels.

1. Go as deep into a stretch as you can and hold for 3–5 seconds.

2. Return to neutral for 3–5 seconds.

3. Repeat for as many reps as necessary for you to feel improve-ment (5–10 is average).

As you move through that process, you should begin to notice that your range (depth of stretch) is likely improving with every repetition. This is because you are increasing the circulation in the area you are stretching, which causes your body to respond rapidly. The old method of holding a stretch for 30+ seconds actually restricts circulation, which means less blood and oxygen to the tissue, and that can get in the way of achieving your desired results.

Focus on Breathing

It sounds simple, but the one thing we all do without thinking about is the one thing we absolutely need to prioritize and focus on. Our breath controls so much of our physiology; it is truly incredible.

There are so many things we can control in our body if we simply pay attention to our breath. We can relax, or we can warm up. We can get energy even more powerful than a cup of coffee in just 30 seconds. The breath really is the gateway to a higher quality of life. Breath can pick you up and energize you in a hurry or help you de-stress and relax in a few seconds.

Try this breathing exercise for relaxation and focus. The speed of the count is up to you, but keep it consistent in all four steps. **Slow is best.**

1. Sitting comfortably, after your next exhale, begin the exercise.

2. Inhale deeply through the nose to the count of four.

3. Hold the air in for the count of four.

4. Exhale through the mouth to the count of four.

5. Hold without air to the count of four.

If you begin to focus on your breathing throughout the day and remember to breathe deeply through the nose into the abdomen and exhale through the mouth, your stress levels will decrease, your focus will increase, and your body will thank you. The benefits of breathing with intention are amplified if you are staying well hydrated and moving your body.

These simple activations will create boundless changes.

Even though this is not a one-size-fits-all approach (and paying attention to your nutrition and sleep will help tremendously), there are two things that, if you do them every day upon waking, will activate everything else.

If you do only these two things, you will be amazed at how much clarity you have and how much you're able to accomplish in a single day.

What are the two things?

1. Drink water.

2. Do wall squats.

That's it. Easy to do (but also easy not to do).

If you want more free ACTIVATION tools as well as special access to activation and leverage retreats, check out the QR code below for additional resources:

ArielAmavi.com

CONCLUSION
Million Dollar Identity

Take a few minutes to think about those figures in our past and present culture whose larger-than-life identity could be felt in any space they entered ... people with messages and stories like Tony Robbins, Mother Teresa, Stephen Hawking, John Paul DeJoria (Paul Mitchell), the Dalai Lama, J.K. Rowling, Henry Ford, and the entrepreneurs who've just shared a piece of their life with you.

Without them saying a word, you can FEEL their presence when they walk into a room. WHO they are is completely intertwined with what they DO. But can they DO things because of BEING who they are? Do they HAVE the influence, the reputation, the power, or the wealth because they have so completely identified with WHY they are here?

But what happens when Identity is ripped away? Imagine if WHO YOU ARE is inseparable from what you DO until circumstances make it impossible for you to continue BEING a soldier, CEO, doctor, wife, lawyer, dad. Do you just "get" a new identity? Or do you delve into hopelessness and depression?

How do you make your way forward again? Hopefully you realize in story after story, at least once, each of our authors experienced this dilemma and it helped shape who they are today—someone with a Million Dollar Identity and the belief that they are exactly where they are meant to be, guiding others on their journeys to achieving hopes and dreams.

What happens when Identity defines your sense of worth, value, or potential? What if your race, socioeconomic standing, childhood circumstances, educational level, or trauma contribute to you identifying as someone who is not deserving of better, of more, of opportunity, or of ease?

Can you change your identity? Or are you forever stuck with a poverty mindset and limiting beliefs? And how do you overcome any insecurities around belonging? As the authors have pointed out, sometimes it takes work, time, effort, and desire. And it always takes finding someone who has gone before you to reach back and show you the way.

Is YOUR identity determined externally or internally? Imagine if your gender is or isn't valued in your culture, your skin color is perceived as positive or negative, or your religion suggests you must act or vote a certain way.

What if you internalized labels? Slow, introvert, non athletic, awkward, not good with numbers, or any other word or phrase that makes you feel less than. Maybe you just always felt like you were different.

Do you claim an identity to fit in or stand out? Leaders choose to stand out, to own their differences, to claim their influence in order to help others build their visibility, credibility, authority, and influence. As our authors have demonstrated, it isn't always easy, and barriers can serve to inspire us to choose to become greater than our obstacles. We may all choose to BE someone with a Million Dollar Identity.

Do you know who you are and why you are here? And has your Identity ever been challenged by events? The APA Dictionary of Psychology defines identity as "an individual's sense of self, defined by (a) a set of physical, psychological, and interpersonal characteristics that is not wholly shared with any other person and (b) a range of affiliations (e.g., ethnicity) and social roles."

A psychological identity relates to self-image, self-esteem, and individuality. Identity development helps you form a view of who you are at a point in time.

To earn $1 million annually, you have to generate $83K per month *every* month. Think about whether or not your identity supports or hinders your capacity to consistently generate high monthly revenue. Is it possible to attain if we have tried before and failed, come from less fortunate beginnings, or if language, gender, or health present barriers to success? If we don't believe we deserve or are capable of financial achievements, if we find ourselves derailed from our path or plans, or if we are confused about who we are or need to become, *is it possible to begin again?* Absolutely. Our authors have proven it on these pages. And that means you can begin again, too!

What would it look and feel like to have or develop a Million Dollar Identity?

- *What Legacy could we leave?*

- *What Movement could we create?*

- *What Impact could we have?*

- *What difference could we make?*

- *Who could we serve?*

- *What problems could we solve?*

- *What pain could we relieve?*

- *What hope could we offer?*

- *Who could we become?*

Our wish for you is that the stories our authors have shared on these pages have encouraged you to believe you are worthy and deserving of all great things. Having a Million Dollar Identity is less dependent on a dollar metric than it is on how you show up in the world, who you choose to learn from, and what you choose to do as a leader of yourself, your audience and team, your family and community.

Reach out to the authors, avail yourself of their heart, their energy, and their offers. Be open to possibilities and take the first step to BECOME your best self, the one who is growing into a Million Dollar Identity!

Thank you for being here. Thank you for reading this book and for your time and attention. Most importantly, thank you for having the courage for wanting to understand what it takes for you to develop *your* Million Dollar Identity.

Be sure to check out the offers our million-dollar authors have made available to you in this book, and beginning today, *your life will be changed!*

ACKNOWLEDGMENTS

I want to start by giving a very special thanks to my business partner, Angela Little. Entrepreneurship can sometimes be a lonely affair. Sure, you meet with your Inner Circle members and speak often with your Mastermind groups, but when it comes to the day in and day out challenges, it's hard to talk to family or friends who support you but don't truly understand what it means to be responsible for carving out your destiny to serve as many other people as you can before time is up. I am so grateful for our daily planning sessions, for your humor, your abundance mindset, and your strength and kindness. We may be separated by an ocean and busy with our own families, but your presence makes all the difference.

I want to thank Russell Brunson and the ClickFunnels community, Bastiaan Slot and the Millionaire Consulting community, Ryan Stewman and the Apex community, Sam Ovens and his community because through these overlapping networks and the leaders within them, I have learned much, been inspired by many, and grown real friendships.

I would be remiss if I didn't call out huge gratitude to a deeply special leader, Dr. Myron Golden. He is a man of high integrity, wisdom, and big vision. He is kind, funny, gentle, yet so very powerful in his presence. He is a beacon for hope and a driver for massive action and even bigger results. He embraces his community with special guidance, and I am sincerely honored that he takes my calls and pushes me toward ever bigger goals.

Finally, I extend deep and heartfelt thanks to the entrepreneur-authors who have shared their journeys on these pages so we may understand there are more similarities than differences on the road to growing into someone with a Million Dollar Identity.

ABOUT JAMIE WOLF AND MILLION DOLLAR STORY AGENCY

Jamie Wolf is the CEO and President of Million Dollar Story Agency. Her purpose is to inspire others to dream big, implement fast, never quit, and stay surrounded with epic, amazing, inspirational humans—always! Jamie and her Agency help experts—entrepreneurs, consultants, speakers, coaches, CEO's and business owners—become #1 bestselling authors on the elite lists to build their brand, visibility, market authority, and credibility. Perhaps even more significantly, she makes sure you write a strategic book—or chapter in an anthology—based on the Million Dollar Method, that addresses all five factors essential to every thriving business: lead gen, lead nurture, lead conversion, client fulfillment, and client retention! The result for you is increased influence, amplified authority, and soaring cash flow once you are intentionally positioned as the 'go-to' person in your niche! As a fierce advocate for people and their stories, she is here to share your stories—just as she has done in this book—so you can expand your influence, audience, revenue, and impact even further. Additionally, Jamie is the founder of Wolf Tide Publishing. A multiple bestselling author herself, Jamie has helped many 6-, 7-, and 8-figure entrepreneurs reach bestseller status and STAY in the Top 25-100 for

12+ months. She has a Master's in Business from Arizona State and was the co-founder of a venture-funded disease-management start-up company that got a medical device through FDA clearance on time and within budget. Next, Jamie is the creator and host of the *Million Dollar PIVOT* podcast. Lastly, Jamie is mom to three amazing adults, rescuer to perhaps too many critters, and lover of the ocean and the outdoors.

Million Dollar Story Agency is a global agency working with entrepreneurs and leaders across industries and verticals to build your brand visibility and market authority. When you share your powerful story, you are truly seen as an extraordinary and remarkable leader, one of the elite and passionate difference-makers!

MillionDollarStory.co

WE HAVE A BIG FAVOR TO ASK. WILL YOU HELP US?

THANK YOU

IF YOU LOVED THIS BOOK LEAVE A REVIEW OR SHARE A PICTURE ON SOCIAL

★ ★ ★ ★ ★

Thank You for Reading *Million Dollar Identity!*

I love hearing your ideas about the book and how you relate to these stories—and how you are taking action! The team at Million Dollar Story Agency wants to know that the stories we tell and produce are making a difference.

Please go to Amazon today, leave a review, and share your thoughts about the book. We genuinely appreciate your time and feedback!

Thanks again!

–Jamie Wolf